THE
WHOLE
METHOD

ISBN: 9781950367085
Published by
Lifestyle Entrepreneurs Press
Las Vegas, NV

Editor: Alli Blair Snyder

If you are interested in publishing through Lifestyle Entrepreneurs Press, write to: Publishing@LifestyleEntrepreneursPress.com

Publications or foreign rights acquisitions of our catalog books.
Learn More: www.LifestyleEntrepreneursPress.com

Printed in the USA

THE
WHOLE
METHOD

RHONDA SMITH

For the leader who's ready to answer the question "what comes next after personal development?" This is an invitation to remember who you really are so that you can lead and inspire the people you serve even more profoundly.

More than ever before people need guidance, as many of the old paradigms to break down and disintegrate.

We've created a free guide and a series of masterclasses to support you as you step into your power and claim your true potential.

Join us in our mission, as we transition through these dark and tumultuous times.

This is about remembering the truth and joining together. The fate of the human species hangs in the balance, will you accept the call?

We've created a free guide and a series of masterclasses to support you as you remember who you really are, step into your power, and unleash your true potential. This is for the leaders that the world needs right now, more than ever. Join us at TheExpandedHueman.com/truth

This book is dedicated to my favorite beings in the world and in the cosmos.

Smith, I couldn't have done any of this without you. You are my best friend and the best father I could have ever asked for. Thank you for teaching me to love life and nature. Thank you for the soft place to land as I sat in my mess and remembered myself. I love you more.

To my amazing family, I love you all dearly. Family is such a gift and I treasure each and every one of you. A special thanks to my sister who has always supported me and loved me unconditionally.

To the most incredible teachers and healers on the planet, thank you for not giving me the answers and for supporting me as I found my way. Nai Kaya, Jeff Murphy, Mark Yegge, Tim Rhode, Bernhard Guenther: it is such a gift to be in all of your lives.

A special thank you to Josh Muscat and Adriane Bovone for the amazing friendship, and for the incredible support of my precarious nervous system.

To my best friends on the planet. I love you all madly. Thank you for helping me understand that true friendship is a special kind of family. I couldn't be more thrilled to celebrate life and create our mission together.

Thank you to Jesse Krieger, Jonathan Gunzel, Julie Ritchie, and Alli Blair Snyder. This book was a collaboration of incredible effort. Thank you all for sharing your genius in this process.

To Scott one of the greatest friends and teachers I have ever known. I don't know where I would be without knowing you; probably running some crazy new-age cult. There are no words.

To the love of my life, Saylor Love: you are the best thing that ever happened to me when with your legendary cuddles and the sweetest love I have ever known. You are my girl forever and ever.

And to Red, the best mama on the planet. Thank you for loving me so fiercely and for teaching me that anything can be figured out. I love you. Ride the winds, magical woman. Let's meet and dance in the breeze.

TABLE OF CONTENTS

THE STORY BEHIND THE STORY

Nothing was working.

After years of personal development, and countless plant medicine ceremonies, I was trying and pushing so hard to build my dream business and ideal life - but it just wasn't happening. I was so fucking frustrated as I watched others appear to have success, and I was still struggling.

What I didn't realize then was that I'd bought into a "dream" that wasn't mine. I was climbing the wrong mountain and chasing someone else's vision! It caused me a lot of suffering.

At my lowest point, I can remember lying on the floor in the fetal position, crying and begging for some answers. But it was only once I fully allowed myself to feel my pain, to sink into the darkness, frustration, and despair, that some healing finally occurred. It wasn't until I finally allowed myself to truly feel that things began to shift.

As I gradually came out of that dark place, the thought occurred to me, "I can't be the only one. There must be others who feel like this."

It turned out, there were!

At the time, I was offering private coaching and retreats; they began to get sold out. One day I was talking to some of the people who'd attended. As I listened to their stories, it became clear that they were feeling just as lost and unfulfilled as I had been.

Some were wearing masks in order to be accepted by their peers. They weren't in touch with their own truth and inner wisdom, so they were trying to create from a place that wasn't aligned, and it felt to them like pushing a boulder up a hill. The entrepreneurs I talked to, especially, felt they were missing a community that really "got" them. They were lonely and exhausted from pretending.

Some felt they didn't have a voice and couldn't speak their truth. Others had created some success in business, but were struggling in their personal lives. Many were living purely for significance and the approval of others, abusing their bodies and privately struggling with addictive tendencies. Yet more still were questioning whether the "western" focus on achievement and progress was harming our living planet in irreversible ways, and were feeling the pain of watching animals suffer. Some were too numbed out to even see the suffering.

All were deeply unfulfilled, despite their impressive achievements.

How could this be? It was like an epidemic of dissatisfaction!

These were the people who were doing regular personal development work. Often, the "put together" exterior we present to the world isn't how we really feel inside.

As we connected more, a group of us began to form. Five of us decided to come together and support each other to find a new way, one where we could marry accomplishment with a deeper meaning. We were all willing to do the work. We were all willing to look within and face our own shadows, and we committed to supporting each other.

As we began to do the work, a transformation occurred naturally in each of our lives. We each experienced very personal, yet very universal, changes. We felt more fulfillment and found more meaning in the everyday. Experiences began to feel richer. We were able to understand what "enough" felt like, whilst still creating together, each following our Dharma.

Our businesses took off and money began to flow more easily. Personal relationships found healing, toxic patterns were released, and our individual health started to flourish. And we all lived happily ever after and everything was perfect!

Not really - things don't go from shit to gold. But things were so much better. We had our community; we had a place to learn and be exactly who and how were. We didn't have to pretend or wear masks anymore. Life is not about living in an elevated state of being happy all the time. For the first time, we really got to show up, be ourselves, and be accepted for who we were when we were raw and naked. You can't believe what happens to a person when they feel whole in who they really are. This level of acceptance and self-responsibility opens us up to our greatest potential.

As we all grew closer and watched our lives really begin to shift, we knew we had to share it with the world. A mission began to unfold, and a new company, The Expanded Hueman, was born.

Our community has since grown, and it is now our mission to extend the invitation to all the souls who are ready.

What if we changed the "dream" and made a new one together? How would that look? What if a critical mass of people joined together? We believe that solutions will begin to appear.

The world doesn't need to be saved, she needs to be loved. People in this world don't need to be saved, they need to be loved. It's only once we do the internal work that the outside circumstances will change.

This book that you are holding in your hands is a necessary part of doing the internal work. Doing the work within a community is the secret, and we've created that community just for you. We invite you to join us.

We've created a series of fucking epic content to support you as you continue the work to remember who you really are, step into the next level of your personal power and unleash your truest potential. This is for you, the leader, to take your mission to more people. As you rise up, you can also support your community and followers to do the same. This creates a ripple effect and a catalyst for real change

Sign up at TheExpandedHueman.com/truth

INTRODUCTION

"*There is nothing to fear in the stillness, except the awakening of your own power.*"

-KIM KRANS

Human: do you yearn for something deep down? I think you do. But you can never quite put your finger on what that something is, can you? It's called to you your entire life, but it still remains a mystery. No matter where you look, it escapes you - like a slippery, moving shadow you catch out of the corner of your eye. It's a mystery that is almost solved in each new endeavor, in each new goal you set, but then is gone like a wisp of smoke that lingers in the air just long enough to smell it. It leaves you with a momentary and fleeting satisfaction that simply makes you want more and more of it – but it never lasts. You find that the more you do, learn, and strive to find and hold onto that feeling, the more you're aware of the void inside when it's gone.

I have news for you, fellow human. What you're seeking isn't found outside of you! What you're seeking is The Truth. When I first began to learn and experience Truth, I didn't know it would forever shift the way I viewed and lived my life. Embracing my personal truth and understanding the "Truth of Life" were the keys that unlocked everything for me. When I started this journey, I was living a high stress lifestyle working in finance. I was riddled with anxiety, addictive tendencies, and neurosis, much like many people in society today; maybe even a lot like you. When my life crashed and burned - when I left my husband, when I lost all my money, and when I became trapped in the downward spiral of addictive tendencies - little did I know, that was when the true healing would begin! I had to break open for my courage to be revealed, which would allow me to face my darkest fears and ultimately begin my path to consciousness.

Today, I am taking each day as it comes and living my Dharma, unafraid of the feelings that have been deemed 'negative' and unafraid of my shadow self. Today I can sit with myself, and all the pieces of me, quite comfortably. I feel more at peace than ever before. My life works; I'm on my path, in my truth. Today, I'm lucky enough to support others in embracing their own Truth in remembering who they really are. As they do so, I witness them unlocking their true potential: an unlimited power source within, as opposed to the "limited power" we usually run from. As I watch my clients go through their transformation, I see them making new discoveries and I see them becoming more themselves. This book is about how to do exactly that: how to become more you, how to stop trying to get from here to there, and how to understand that what you are looking for is found in the mystery of the present as it unfolds. This book is for the leader who knows, deep down inside, that there is a different way. It's for the leader who is connected to the idea that there is a different dream, one that will regenerate and create a more balanced existence between all life on earth and with the living earth herself. It's for you if you've already done a lot of sincere self-work and are ready to really understand what this is all about. This book is for you if you're looking for the Truth.

Every step of the journey to get to today was mine to take; no one could do it for me. Waiting within each new experience was the information I needed for the next step along the way. But this journey wasn't about reaching a destination; it was about learning to deeply experience each new moment, richly and thoroughly. It was about becoming present, embodied, and appreciative of what was right in front of me, rather than judging it as "lacking" or rushing to get onto the next thing. Waiting within every breath was another opportunity to become naked with who I really am and how I relate to the world. When I was able to accept myself fully and embrace every piece of me, that was when my life changed, and my own true potential was unleashed. The most incredible thing is that it was far beyond anything I could ever have imagined. The realization that our potential is limitless blows my mind each and every day. This is what's possible for all of us when we're able to truly be ourselves; when we peek through the veil, look past the version of life that we've been sold, and see the Truth.

This is what I invite you to do. The fire that burns in our untamed souls has a quest for us that's bigger than anything we can imagine. Our miraculous life offers unlimited possibilities - the perfect blend of challenges, obstacles, and bliss - to help us uncover the magic that's waiting within. But, among other reasons, the way that our world is currently structured is blocking us from tapping into this potential within. Systems keep us down; conditioning and hostile forces slow our progress. Humanity is currently on a course that will ultimately result in our end and the destruction of our home, Mother Earth. Unless we change something, together.

The good news is that we're in a time of a great shift: humanity is finally beginning to wake up from a long slumber, and we have the ability to pivot the path we've been on. We've been on a blind, unconscious quest for "the dream," but now we have a chance to choose a new dream, one we imagine for ourselves; one that is more aligned with our souls and the evolution of humanity. But to do so, we must trek through our past traumas, shine light into all the dark corners of ourselves that we've preferred not to look at and embrace our shadow selves. Only then can we become "Whole." This is true enlightenment. The secret is to not become distracted by the shiny objects and riches that have been programmed into humanity as "the dream." There's something far greater for us to experience than the external over-consumption which has been encouraged in our society, and the fleeting validation that comes from more "stuff."

All that we seek is within us. For most of us, we simply don't remember the way back into ourselves to find it. To sit and listen to the intelligence of our own being can feel threatening. I'm not referring to the quiet that we experience in meditation; I'm talking about exploring the depth of our feelings and fears. To be with ourselves. To allow ourselves to sit in the truth of our experiences and listen to the sacred wisdom that is held there when we are present. What if that something we've been seeking all this time is actually waiting patiently for us in the shadows of our own feelings? My own potential was waiting in the darkness of my fears and in the space between my tears. We live in a world that teaches us to constantly "change our state" rather than listen to the truth of what we truly feel at the moment. We're taught that we don't need to deal with those pesky "negative" emotions, instead we paint rainbows over the top of them and change them into the "positive" feelings we prefer to experience. Many people numb their pain with anything from sex, masturbation, food, alcohol, and drugs to shopping, serial dating, and working themselves to the bone. I kept myself busy and distracted for many years in the name of productivity, success, and my need to be seen while avoiding the wisdom and truth that was waiting quietly within me.

When we do sit in the quiet of our truth, it can bring up deep feelings of loneliness. For some it is terrifying to be alone, to simply be left with ourselves and our experiences. To truly be comfortable with being alone, we have to have made peace with ourselves and with reality. We must embrace the fact that it's up to us to create our own experience and take responsibility for our lives and our acceptance levels about what is. It's important to make the distinction between being lonely and simply being alone. Being lonely is a state of mind based on a thought pattern. When I didn't understand this, extreme loneliness drove me to do all kinds of things that weren't in my best interest over and over again. It was this repetitive cycle that kept me in my irresponsible patterns of behavior and addictive tendencies. Being able to sit with our feelings of loneliness gives us the freedom to create something different for ourselves. From this deeper place, we can begin to connect with that fire inside and finally hear our own guiding wisdom.

For many of us, the need to be seen and acknowledged is brought to the surface in the quest for external validation. My own quest for approval drove me to betray myself. It pushed me to take actions that were out of alignment with me and my deepest Truth. My desperation to be seen and loved in romantic relationships led me to partners who were emotionally unavailable. The dysfunctional way in which I'd learned to express love was to choose partners from my wounded self. From my victim perspective at the time, it seemed to me that I chose men with narcissistic tendencies who would show me love at first and then take it away to replace it with cruelty or indifference. I now see it differently and own my experience. I realize that my own core wounds of severe codependency and my need to be seen by these men kept me in a vicious holding pattern, where I allowed myself to remain in a state of victimhood. This repetitive experience undermined my self-worth and was the catalyst to me trying to take my own life more than once. These were my lowest points. Thankfully, I was unsuccessful, and it was the wake-up call I needed.

I realized that this destructive pattern would never end until I figured out how to see and love myself. I couldn't rely on another person to do it for me! My resistance to loving myself the way I wanted others to love me was some of my hardest work. Once I understood this, I was able to take ownership of my experiences of life and of love. I was better able to see my path ahead, my way out of suffering, and the steps I needed to take. I now firmly believe that this part of my journey was designed for my soul's evolution. Our need to be acknowledged by those who we deem important is an indicator that we're not seeing ourselves. This learning of how to see ourselves the way we'd like others to see us takes time. It takes practice; it is the work of our lives.

We're so busy endlessly seeking answers outside of ourselves, searching for answers to questions we've been taught to ask, that we never check whether they are the right questions! We hold the belief that we must receive the answers from other people, but we never think to look inside ourselves for the truth first. We're often taught that the answers we seek can be found by buying into the quest for "success" and the pursuit of "knowledge." We buy programs, books, courses, and retreats. The ultimate goal is to produce more.

There's an unspoken agreement that the more we consume and produce, the more successful we will be. To make more money, buy more stuff, move into a bigger house. "If you're not growing, you're dying," say the personal-development gurus. But everything has a season. When did we become so disconnected from nature as to think that this doesn't apply to us? We are part of the cyclical nature of life, not knowing that the very pursuit of knowledge and success itself is what's keeping us from what we're looking for. My own endless pursuit to gain knowledge and success, coupled with the belief that I could not figure it out myself, caused me to pull out my credit card, over and over again. Grabbing every opportunity that could possibly be the thing that could be the answer for me and my life. But it never was. I created my life from a space of lack, always searching for more.

I've learned that when we truly understand ourselves, know our truth, and have embraced the parts of ourselves that we've spent a lifetime running from, we create from a different place inside. Our life is fueled from a different consciousness, one of acceptance and true "service to others" contribution rather than consumption. The result of our being this way far exceeds the efforts we put forth in all of our previous doing. This doesn't imply that we simply sit and wait for it all to happen. It's the understanding that the quality of our being dictates our results, that where we create from holds the key, and our state of being ripples out through the ethers to the larger world out there. If we create from the place of an unconscious ego, that feeds unhealthy desires and keeps us perpetually in a state of not having enough, it keeps us from seeing the parts of ourselves that desperately need to find healing. When we have peace inside, we are able to just "be." When we're able to be with the truth, to be with ourselves and to accept what is, right now, we are able to understand our Dharma.

The Whole Method isn't about following some prescribed step by step formula to find what you're seeking. This book offers something far more valuable. It offers insight to help you remember your way back to yourself. To remember who and what you really are. To remember the truth. Because there are no two paths that are the same, so how can there be one formula for everyone? When you are on the path to Wholeness, you stop blindly following the trail that was never meant for you. It's about reconnecting with your own internal compass and blazing your own magnificent trail. From this place, we are able to tap into our truest, unlimited potential. When I started listening to my own internal compass, that's when life really took off for me. Here is where it can for you too, if you're ready for the truth inside. Are you ready to find what's been calling to you all along?

CHAPTER 1:
THE CALLING

"Hoarding a library full of books you've never read is hoarding knowledge others could learn from and is like hoarding a bank account full of dollars you will never spend."

-LAMA NORBU

The warm breeze whispered across my face and woke me up. The first few seconds of the morning, when there is no memory of the reality of life, are a fleeting gift. I opened my eyes and pulled myself out of bed; deep feelings of loneliness began to move through my nerves, but were quickly muted by the chemicals that coursed through my being. As I took my first full step out of bed, I tripped over the endless stacks of magazines and piles of newspapers that covered the floor. I don't read them; they are a collection of important events in history that seem to matter to a lot of people. I planned to sell them online one day, but I hadn't gotten around to it. As I turned sideways to squeeze by the unopened boxes of items purchased online in the early morning hours of loneliness, I was reminded that there was no room left for me to live here.

There were several paths that allowed me to move through the chaos. They felt like small tunnels rats move through to go where they must. There was a path from my front door to where I slept; it was more where

I laid and spent my time glued to a screen rather than sleeping. Next to my bed was the charging station for my screen, the hub of my existence when I was home. Once I made it through my room and into the bathroom, I opened the medicine cabinet and took my daily pill, which kept me from feeling the *truth* of my life. A more accurate description would be that it held the truth back enough so I could function in this world. Sometimes, I believe it was the thing that kept me feeling sick, in an existence filled with empty "likes" and the quest for fame and money. In my village, we were all living for the life portrayed on the screens; earning money in order to consume more things and goods so we could feel better about our empty lives. Meanwhile, the people selling the goods made more and more money, so they could buy more things too. It was an endless circle.

I followed the path to the kitchen that wasn't exactly a kitchen in the way that I used it; it was where I stored most of the things I bought. It was filled to the brim with hand-made baskets, silk robes of all colors, empty pill containers, and boxes of stuff I thought I might need one day. Somewhere in there was an assortment of gadgets to keep my screens working, but I've never been able to find them. Standing in that kitchen, I felt deep down that I was lonely and starving for real connection. There were many people living in my village, each numbed by pills and living life for the "likes;" existing for consumerism. Our screens gave us the opportunity to be more connected than ever before, yet we were all more lonely than ever. I walked toward my bed and put on the same clothes I wore the day before. This was always easier than finding and choosing different ones. My stomach grumbled, and I realized it was time for breakfast. I headed into our village to get some food.

Everyone in my small village was living the same numbed-out life; their edges had all been roughed down, so we were all kind of the same on the outside. Most people wore the same clothing, so it became difficult to tell anyone apart. The culture was that of ousting things that were different; it was better to blend in. There was a lot of fear of the unknown and of what was beyond the edge of the village. The fears and superstitions included the belief that if we kept the fires burning for light, they would ward off any forest creatures that lingered in the dark. Forests were being decimated to keep the fires burning, but no one seemed to care. The villagers consume so many things; they keep cutting down more trees to build more places to store their stuff. No one seems to understand that we are using up our natural resources. It is as though fueling the fires in the name of our fear, numbing our feelings, and feeding our need for consumerism is more important than our resources and the earth.

With my numbed-out gaze, I looked around the small plaza where we lined up for food. I saw the dazed villagers walking with heads down in different directions while staring at screens in their hands. Everyone was everywhere bumping into each other, but no one was talking; they moved silently on their way to grab a sea to get deeper into their screens. Everyone was going through the motions of existence, but no one was seeing what was around them, much less the person right next to them. I followed a group to get in line for "chow;" my body sighed as if it knew it was going to be fed the nutritional value of cardboard. Empty calories pretended to keep me full but offered no nourishment for my mind or my body. Despite the lack of taste and nourishment in the so-called food, the line was exceptionally long. The desire to grow food and cook a meal was no longer part of our ways. No matter what we consumed, we couldn't fill the emptiness. The villagers would consume anything they could to try and appease themselves. It wasn't their fault; they lacked the ability to connect with the things that would make them whole. Even though I lived this way for a long time, I somehow felt a separation from them. As though something inside of me was different.

Over years of societal breakdown, the minds and hearts of the villagers grew cold and unaware. Their minds were consumed by desire, and their hearts were lost. In the confusion, the ways of the ancestors were lost too. The villagers forgot that family is the purest form of human relations. Those who left this village were never heard from again. Some believe they were called by the whispers of the trees. The whispers promised a life of bounty, success, and riches. There were no whispers coming to me, and each day was the same as the last. I was numb inside, but there was an itch that kept telling me there was more. I thought maybe it was just a side effect of my pill wearing off.

Strolling through the plaza, I gazed at the fine things the merchants had for sale. This was the only time my heart felt anything, but the feeling was short-lived. I made my way to my favorite stretch of the plaza, the area with fine handcrafted things. Silk robes were sold in every color. Beautiful pottery was sold but never used. I saw the same villagers wanting the same things in a different color every day. I was no different. I had all the things in every color, yet I couldn't resist the idea of having one more in the event I wanted to use it one day. People in the village were walking around carrying their new things, hoarding their purchases, as though having these things made them royalty. The most intricately woven hand-baskets were on the edge of the plaza and I was always called to the table where they were displayed. Even though I attempted to be frugal, I couldn't help but buy a new basket when one caught my eye. My overflowing kitchen told a different story about my efforts toward being frugal - but what the heck, what was one more?

I purchased a handbasket with a strong handle and geometric patterns seamlessly wrapped around the exterior of the basket. As I walked away, the rush of the purchase shuffled me home. I placed my new basket next to the others; I couldn't help but feel the rush fading. I wished the feeling would linger a bit longer, or that I could feel the rush more often, but my pocketbook didn't allow it. I sat, surrounded by baskets and colorful robes that had no use to me, and longed for something more. I looked for my bottle so I could take another pill. I took more than one pill on a lot of days. I wasn't sure I was supposed to, but I did it anyway. These pills helped me *not* to feel anything, yet through the deep waves of numbness, I still felt an emptiness in my soul. As I popped another pill, I decided I could not keep living this way. I spit it out. I knew there must be something more. I mouthed the words, "Universe, please let me hear the whispers."

A gust of wind burst the shutters open and the sound startled me so much I fell over; the baskets and robes went flying. Laying on the ground covered in my things, I could hear the wind blowing through the leaves. The energy of the wind was so strong I couldn't deny its force. Its presence was intense, almost as though it was staring me in the face. Out of nowhere, I heard a voice telling me to listen. I looked around to see where it was coming from, but there was no one there. I listened and heard a faint whisper. It told me I could have all I desired. Was this the whisper that offered the call for the riches of life? I looked at all the things I had purchased, trying to feel better, but I felt only emptiness. From the stories I'd heard, I knew I must leave most everything behind to follow these whispers. There was a brief moment when I wanted to hold onto the life I had been living. It was empty, but familiar. I had been numb enough to continue this way for a long time.

Then, a voice inside of me told me that when we listen to the whispers they lead us to where we are meant to be. As I looked at my screen, an intense sensation of panic came over me. In this moment, I knew that to have a different life, one with purpose, I had to cut cords with the things that kept me tethered. I thought of all the things I would miss. My screen was my companion, as long as it had "juice" I was occupied. What would happen to me if I wasn't connected to it? When I decided to set the screen down and leave it behind, I felt a deep sense of peace. I hoped I would be able to find a life without being connected to it. I packed my favorite bag with the things I thought I needed; I grabbed my little purse filled with gold coins. It was all the money I had in the world. I took out one coin, put it in my pocket, and tucked the rest inside my bag. I stepped out the door toward my life. I looked back to see the reality I had been living. I left the door open with the intention of never coming back. It had been my home, filled with all of my things, yet I felt no sadness about leaving it behind. In that moment I felt something deep inside me that had been dormant - a spark that would fuel me on my path. The time had come for me to find a new way. It was the first time, in a very long time, that I remember a feeling that lasted more than a fleeting second.

I walked to the furthest trace of the village, an old fence made of crumbling stone, while the villagers stared at my retreating back. The daylight began to fade and my sense of direction was altered. I couldn't find my way back to that crumbling fence if I tried. I stopped to rest and eat some food; I didn't have a lot to sustain me. I could barely see a clearing ahead; I hurried there in hopes of finding a place to rest. The darkness consumed the light and the leaves began to whisper. The longer I listened, the more I realized they were actual voices. As the last bit of light was fading, I could see people sitting in the grass wearing simple robes. The wind whispered for me to get closer. Running out of food and things in my bag, I hoped these people would give me some direction. When I approached them, they did not have much to say. I looked for a connection in their faces, but their stares were as blank as the villagers'. I asked if they heard the whispers in the trees and if they knew the way. They replied with a simple nod and a sense of tranquility. They asked what I was willing to pay to know the way. I reached into my pocket and rubbed the gold coin I had put there earlier. As I pulled it out, I hoped it would be enough to get me on my way. They accepted the coin and pointed to a trail ahead. Their long fingers extended to the tops of the trees, where the peak of a mountain could be seen. I had lived here my whole life and never noticed any mountains.

●

Knowledge is power, but no one really *owns* knowledge. True knowledge is free and available to anyone with a keen enough eye to know where to look for it. Most people still question the idea that they already have everything they need to find their way inside of them, so they search for an external compass, or system, to guide them. This is linked to the insidious concept that there's a quick fix or shortcut to where you want to go, *if only you could find it!* You may come to believe that to achieve greatness, you must pay for it. I myself often paid handsomely for it. Too often the information I bought was regurgitated and convoluted. Is there really any new information out there? Further, do we allow ourselves time to fully integrate and practice the new information we take in? Knowledge combined with integration is wisdom.

That itch inside, the thing that calls to your soul, has an appetite that is always ravenous. The interesting part is that I am not sure if we know what the hunger is, or what it's truly ravenous for. So we keep feeding it, but it remains under-nourished despite a constant diet of over-consumption. In our quest to understand this hunger inside, we pay our fee to feast at the table of truth and knowledge, *or what is perceived to be truth and knowledge.* We sit down and we pick up our wooden spoon. As we begin to gorge ourselves on the information we've been told will fill us, we observe those around us also gorging at a rapid rate. We begin to consume even more information to try and keep up; more books, more podcasts, more programs, more gurus, more masters, *more bullshit.*

We've taken in so much information, so many systems, and thought processes, that we no longer have time to think our own thoughts or hear our own wisdom. We aren't listening to the wisdom of our soul; we're listening for *more* information to aid in our pursuit of success. The most devastating part of this level of consumption is there's no time to integrate the knowledge we've gained into our lives. I consumed over twenty books in one year trying to achieve an undefined level of success. In the end, I found I'd consumed a bunch of knowledge I didn't use because it hadn't been integrated. I'd spent all this time listening or reading and found myself more agitated and overwhelmed than ever. What I really needed to do was unpack my backpack of new information and allow some of it to sink in and influence me.

There are one thousand four hundred and forty minutes a day. If we spend most of our waking hours consuming everyone else's information, when do we listen to the brilliant, intuitive, and personalized wisdom that resides deep within our own soul?

Not integrating the knowledge you read makes it as if you never read the book in the first place. It's simply a position of status (to say you're an avid reader) and part of our need to be *seen*. Eventually, we may achieve some of our goals, but not at a fast-enough rate to satisfy the hunger inside. We invest more money into new and better programs, creating debt, with the idea that it will pay off in the end. When we achieve some level of the dream, we realize *this still isn't it*. That deep longing in the soul still isn't satisfied.

My own false dream became obvious when I realized I was affirming something that wasn't true for me. I was pretending to live in a visualized state (fake it till you make it) of what I wanted rather than what was actually true. I was telling myself "I am rich" and "I am successful" when in reality I was ignoring the truth of my life and not tending to the needs of those present moments. As a result, I was missing out on the important information held in those spaces. There's knowledge waiting in our truth. When we tell life that what it has brought us isn't enough, and we need more or something different, *we are completely missing the gift we are given by living in the present*. In every moment we choose to live in the present, we gain the information that's waiting right there to help us grow. If we try to bypass the now, we miss it and can get stuck, or we simply miss the learning. This bypass and desire to *live in the future* is what creates a cycle of disease and a lack of comfort in the present. No one wants to be left with what is real, so instead we seek the stimulation of a different (visualized) reality. This is one of the biggest betrayals of the soul. Our imaginations are wonderful and powerful, but real life only ever happens in the present moment. While finding the delicate balance between our potential to create and imagine, our ability to live in the present is the key.

This is when I began to ask myself the important questions. What is the purpose of it all, and why am I really here? There's no denying we have gained new knowledge and habits throughout this journey. Some level of the information we were gorging on has sunk in, but the quest for more grows stronger and the ability to integrate that knowledge wanes. We become addicts. It drives an even deeper desire to pursue achievement. We cannot ignore the fact that we're growing tired and weary, and we're still not where we think we should be. We do not want to admit this, but we begin to question what we are actually striving for. There has to be more to life than this, because I still haven't found what I'm looking for!

The huge irony about this quest to *seek* and *consume* is that the seeking itself is actually preventing us from receiving what the soul is ravenous for. Instead of "awakening" it from the inside, we just keep feeding it from the outside world of illusion, so it's never really nourished. The quest is the block. We're doing what everyone says we should be doing, but we're not progressing the way we want, and we have a deep level of dissatisfaction gnawing at us. I had the misconception that the process of awakening and the quest for success were one and the same. They're not! For example, some of the "pseudo-spiritual gurus" have made spirituality out to be about financial abundance and fame, stating that we somehow have the ability to manifest all that we desire. We may or may not have this ability; however, do we have the wisdom to use it responsibly if we do? Do we choose to manifest our personal desires, or do we choose to co-create with Spirit?

We come to the time in the journey when we feel as though we're not moving forward with any real purpose. Our previously unwavering belief that what our gurus and teachers were telling us was true begins to come undone. We begin to straddle two worlds, one foot in each: one world is the world of striving for success, of creating, being, and having *more, more, more*. It's the world of being Insta-famous, taking selfies, and posting videos of drinking champagne to social media. It's the world our coaches and mentors have been pushing us to step into. The other world is the quieter internal world, the world of our soul. This world whispers to us, calling us to alignment, embodiment, being present, experiencing, and to a place of enough-ness.

The drive for great wealth and success starts to feel empty. Sometimes there's a crack in the facade, a chink in the armor; at other times, the unconscious ego is hungry, and we go on auto-pilot into all our old habits. Slowly we start to question the entire concept that created our quest in the first place. *Was this quest created from an unconscious ego?* You have what others want, and yet you're still so unfulfilled. What gives? You're blocked and unable to fully connect with what was previously moving you forward. Your mind is blank and in the quiet moments, you realize that you cannot continue on this path unquestioned. *Maybe the time has come to stop seeking.*

"How can I stop?" you wonder. The idea is terrifying; because without seeking, who will you be? You will no longer be able to define yourself by what you're producing or the money you've made. And then what? We live in a society that must be moving and forging ahead all the time. "If you're not growing, you're dying," say the self-development gurus again. But in the name of capitalism, consumption, and growth, we are destroying the only home we have ever known; we're destroying our precious planet. All in an unquestioned mission that may not even be our truth. This "progress" annually lays waste to tens of millions of acres of arable soil to slash and burn agriculture. We don't yet know the true repercussions of the degradation and loss of biodiversity of our great forests. At the same time, we are losing so much ancestral knowledge of plants, and potentially lifesaving plant medicines, all in the name of profitability and the pursuit of success.

Today we're in a time of great quickening. The truth of our actions and the consequences of our disconnection with our Mother Earth are being displayed right before our eyes if we choose to see it. There's a threat to all life on our planet (us included). There are forces far greater than we could ever imagine, working through us and threatening our very existence. But we also have an opportunity, should we choose to take it. If we choose to WAKE UP and see the truth, we have the chance to make peace with life, the earth, and to once again claim our place as *part* of it - not as separate, aloof beings. By simply beginning to discern our quest and our motivating drivers, we'll begin an expansion that's far greater than we could ever imagine. We can begin to hear the whispers that are all around, but will we pause the pursuit and our constant exterior seeking long enough to listen? We must; the time is now.

CHAPTER 2:
THE NEW AGE AND THE
QUEST FOR RICHES

"Free from desire we realize the mystery,
caught in desire we only see the manifestation."
- LAO TZU

I was almost able to smell the money in the air as I began the trek up a steep incline. I was given a compass and told to follow those who'd gone before me because it was "the way." Everything my soul desired would be found at the top of this mountain. Once I conquered the mountain, I would be famous and have great wealth and success. This is the path the whispers had brought me to. It was laced with desire and fulfillment.

The path was well worn from those who'd trodden it before me. There wasn't a tree or shrub in sight, as the people had been burning them to fuel their dreams and desires. In fact, I saw from this height that the mountain was pretty bleak; but there were glimpses of something sparkling in the distance. It was hidden in the undergrowth, where most wouldn't think to look. These sparkles hinted at riches and gems to be found. The people didn't even notice how stripped the mountain had become because they were walking around hyper-focused on their own future goals and desires.

It was as though they were wearing virtual reality goggles, showing up to table after table to feast on more knowledge.

Climbing the mountain seemed an impossible feat, but I convinced myself it needed to be done. My body was detoxing from the pills. I was drenched in sweat and feeling weak. I encountered many souls along the trail who would never make it to the top, exhausted and weary, resigned to sitting on the sides of the path. They settled in their places, selling what they could reap from the mountain in order to survive, further contributing to the degradation of the landscape. I had the urge to grab my screen and take photographs to post my progress on the mountain, but I'd left it behind. I was also detoxing from my screen; it felt as though a part of me was missing. The path was long and wound precariously, but I found a kick in my step because the masters, gurus, and healers I met along the way claimed they knew the secret to great wealth and happiness. They claimed they could heal the parts of me that needed healing. At this point in my journey, I bought into the notion that only others could heal me, and I didn't know I had the ability to heal myself.

As I walked, it became clear that knowledge must be paid for, so I kept giving gold from my purse as my stores dwindled. The more I invested emotionally and physically, the more I felt as though I wasn't going anywhere. The number of things I needed to buy kept growing. People along the path held out special elixirs and potions made with golden honey, claiming they would offer the deepest support with my journey. Some were selling bottles of air they said would bring great awareness. The more that was offered, the more I felt the need to spend. It all began to make me very dizzy and I felt overwhelmed with the task of keeping up. I kept seeing the same landmarks and wondered, "Am I walking around and around in circles here?" It was a continuous loop of seeking.

Finally, I reached a plateau on the mountain, another level in the never-ending game. I was so worn down by the grind that I hardly noticed my progress, not even celebrating that I was standing where I thought I wanted to be. I bought into the idea that I needed to change my state and force myself to think positively, even when I didn't truly feel that way. I became adept at mastering the tools the gurus were preaching - enticing me to change my thoughts, force a positive mindset, and stay the course. They promised they would reveal more secrets for the right price. The higher the level of knowledge, the higher the cost. The price of ascension wasn't cheap, but the yearning in my soul was still there. I couldn't stop now.

Sometimes feelings of doubt would creep into my mind; a yearning deep inside of me was still hungry. In fact, it was growing more ravenous by the day. "How can this be?" I wondered. I've put everything I have into this journey and I still don't feel the way I desire to feel. I began to question the journey itself and started to wonder if I would ever find what I was looking for. Then I caught myself! *My teachers would be so disappointed.* I quickly "changed state" and began to force positivity again. I made a real effort and connected back into all the new-age thinking I'd paid so handsomely for. "What you focus on, you attract." Right?

Yet that feeling inside, that deep hunger in my soul, was beginning to feel like anger and sadness. Something wasn't right. My body was growing tired and my mind was growing weary, but I thought I had to keep going. "*This isn't real,*" I told myself, "*Just change state.*" The body is meant to be hacked! I ignored what my body was trying to tell me and I kept going, forcing myself onwards against all my intuition. I was envisioning the future and the life I wanted. Visualization was the key. What I wanted could only come from remaining in a positive state. I said my affirmations in an attempt to convince my mind, body, and spirit of something that wasn't true, just because I wanted it to be true. I told myself that I was in complete control.

The sun was hot, my body was tired, and I was heavy with frustration and anger. Caught in my visions of the future, I wasn't paying attention to what was in front of me. I lost my footing and was thrown onto the hard path. During my fall I dropped my compass and it shattered on the jagged rocks. With tears streaming down my face, I picked myself up and dusted off. I was bloody and dirty, but no closer to my destination. My compass, my external way-finder that had been guiding my journey up to this point, was now destroyed. When I tripped my coins fell out of my pocket and scattered off the rocky ledge, disappearing down the mountain. I scurried after them like a famished rat after rotten cheese. I caught a glimmer of them in the sunlight as they fell to the bottom of the mountain and into the river.

Desperate, I looked to the masters and gurus that I'd paid to help me along the way. They shook their heads and turned away. They were no longer able to sell me knowledge, because I had no money. Anger reared up inside me. I felt lost and confused. I thought, "How did this happen? I have no compass, and I have no one to help me find the way." I stared into the distance, hoping an answer might materialize from thin air. Suddenly, all of the feelings I'd been pushing and stuffing down began to rise up. I tried to pretend they weren't there, still clinging desperately to an iota of control, but they flooded over me. I had no idea what to do. Hanging my head in defeat, I sat down on the mountainside and let the tears run down my cheeks. I made a sorry picture there; filthy, caked in dried blood, muddied from head to toe, and bawling uncontrollably.

As the sun began to set I saw something glinting in the distance. I wiped the tears from my eyes and squinted so I could see. Something was shining on the horizon, but I didn't know what it was. Sitting up, I peered closer and saw a mountain in the distance. I'd never seen this particular mountain before because I'd had blinders on in order not to be distracted from my quest. There were many mountains in my expanded view and as I gazed along the landscape something kept drawing me back to this one. As my eyes focused, I felt a twinge in my heart and a whisper from my Soul. I realized it was the most beautiful mountain I'd ever seen, and something in my heart clicked! Even from this distance, I could see that wildflowers danced in the meadows and the trees stood valiantly on the ridgelines. "That is my mountain!" I felt it.

With the last moments of daylight, I looked for trails or roads that led across to that mountain, but there weren't any. As far as I could tell, this peak was uncharted territory and the only way to get there would be to blaze my own trail. The idea seemed impossible with no compass and no money to pay for guidance. "There's no way to get there," I thought. *I must stay the course I am on.* I fell into a disturbed and restless sleep, exhausted by the events of the day. In fitful dreams, I saw my mountain and felt a sense of yearning. In my dream state, I'm struggling to reach the mountain, but it never gets any closer and I'm always pulled back. I'm at a crossroads. My mind is telling me to go one way and the other leads where my Soul yearns to explore.

The next morning I woke and again set out to try and find my way, on the mountain I'd been told would bring me happiness. As the hours passed and the day grew hotter, I fatigued and had to stop for a break. I don't normally need to stop for a break. Something was different! Why was I slowing down so quickly? Slowly it dawned on me - the passion I'd been carrying to reach this dream was no longer there. I felt completely hopeless and ready to quit. The people I'd been paying to guide me had inflated my ego with false inspiration, selling me a dream that wasn't mine, but that kept me on the path that paid them. I was alone at first, but I began to find a sense of my freedom in this realization.

I expected to be rewarded with great riches and abundance, but I'd been on the wrong path all along! Powerful emotions began to fill my body. They were so intense I couldn't bear it. I dropped to my knees as a rush of hot anxiety threatened to overcome me. I rolled onto my side as my emotions tore through me like a tornado, ripping me wide open. The only thing that made it bearable was to curl up in the fetal position, holding my knees to my chest and rocking. There was no escaping what was coming, and I cried and raged for hours. This was bigger than me, an outpouring, like a fierce volcano, of all the emotions I didn't know I was capable of feeling and had apparently suppressed. My Truth was finally ready, and there was nothing to do except let it be heard. As my feelings took over, I understood they were filled with information and knowledge. I'd been so busy trying to "force a state" of positivity, I'd missed out on the sacred intelligence trying to come through me. My awareness of my connection to Spirit was exponentially deepened at that moment, and it was all I could do to understand what was happening. It was almost like trying to translate a language I didn't speak, but my body knew the language.

My thinking began to expand, and I began to ask myself questions I'd never thought to ask before: "Why am I here? What is this really about? Am I here for something greater than my personal desires? Why have I been taught that I'm not enough? I've always heard that all I seek is found within, could I, in fact, guide myself?" I began to understand there was great intelligence in my own body, which I'd never been taught to listen to. All this time I thought the body was meant to be a workhorse that served the mind. But now I wondered, "Did the body hold sacred intelligence I wasn't aware of? Are life and happiness really about success and wealth? I need to have certain needs fulfilled, but do I need this excess?" The green, wildflowered mountain in the distance kept coming to mind, and I knew deep in my heart the mountain was calling to my Soul.

At that moment my quest changed. It was no longer about simply achieving wealth, status, and becoming successful; there was something else I needed to discover. I had no idea what I would find, but a new direction called to me. I had no choice but to listen for the first time in my life. There were no expectations, just an unwavering hunger inside of me that knew it was ready to be filled. The calling of the Soul wasn't a choice; it was the quiet voice that's been calling me all along. The one I'd been drowning out with all my "busy" activity. I had to quiet my mind of all the outside noise and learn how to be with my feelings to finally hear it. Dharma called me to step forward and move ahead into the wild unknown. The whispers of my Soul were there the entire time. I chose to answer the call and headed in the direction of my new mountain. I felt nervous about the unknown ahead, but there was also a deep sense of calm grounding me. I thought maybe this first mountain was a test; that everyone here had to realize this for themselves. I was in that realization. With no guidance, no money, and no trail for my tired feet to follow, I wondered if I was crazy, but there was a fire in my belly that wouldn't let me turn back. With this newfound connection with myself, I marched onward in my journey.

●

Why are we afraid to listen to the calling of our Soul? We are distracted by the new age and the quest for riches, so we ignore the whispers of our hearts. We pretend we don't hear the Truth that our whole being knows deep down. We ignore the call, but it becomes louder and louder until finally, it becomes deafening. Somewhere along the way we were taught that to be spiritual means we can have all that we desire; we create our own reality (removed from our surroundings and environment). We all want to save the world, but the world doesn't want to be saved, she wants to be loved. Instead of turning our energy outside of ourselves to create change, we need to focus internally and do the work. When everyone does sincere self-work, that's when humanity will shift.

We believe we have total control over our lives and that we know what's best. Often though, it's the unconscious ego that's in control. We move forward with incredible focus and tunnel vision on our "goals." Forcing our way through life to what we believe is meant for us, focusing only on the manifestation of our personal desires, and completely missing the Mystery that surrounds us; it's simply waiting for us to be present and to listen. In this place, we'll find intelligence and wisdom waiting to be remembered.

"Purpose" is what we think we are here to do. But often, our purpose is out of alignment. Striving for purpose is part of the early path to awakening. It's a spark that quickly becomes a trap, propelling us forward because it feeds the ego and the mind. For me, this was the only way I could listen to the initial call and begin to hear the whispers of my Soul. But it didn't take me long to understand the quest for purpose was a never-ending loop, all the while feeding my ego. The quest was about financial and social gains; the idea that you will be rewarded for all the things you've overcome or that you're somehow entitled to something here on earth. The truth is, we're entitled to nothing.

We are taught from the beginning that life is about the quest for happiness. and there is a method for achieving it. Create success and great wealth and you will be happy - but is this true? The quest to have and become more has been portrayed as the dream, but who came up with this dream? James Truslow Adams defined the expression, "The American Dream," as, "The dream of a land in which life should be better and richer and fuller for everyone, with the opportunity for each according to their own ability for achievement."

It's said all humans are created equal, but I believe this to be a misconception. We are all so drastically unique, we could never be equal. This uniqueness inherently creates inequality and proves not every person has the ability to achieve the same results or the same dream. As seeking humans, we are in a constant state of evolution. We buy into the notion that we will fulfill that deep internal yearning when we achieve this dream. It's been proven time and again, amongst wildly successful individuals and celebrities, that happiness has no correlation to monetary wealth and achievement. Additionally, this dream is exclusive to the first world only. It is not easily available to those who live in the third world or developing countries. Not necessarily available to anyone, except the privileged in the first world and western culture. If you observe the world and listen carefully to those who have achieved this dream, you'll notice what you're seeking isn't found here. It's not an automatic result of more money, power, or fame. Those with eyes willing to see begin to realize the truth we are seeking, the incessant quest for money, power, and fame, got us into trouble in the first place.

A Buddhist story demonstrates this point well: A very wealthy man goes to the monastery asking for a teaching from the Great Master. Upon arrival, the man asks the monk to teach him because he has all this money, but has never truly been happy. The monk simply replies that he cannot help him. The man leaves in dismay. He returns a week later with beautiful and bountiful offerings for the monastery and surrounding villages.

The monk thanks the man graciously, but then replies, "I still cannot help you."

It isn't that he won't help him; it's simply that he can't. Yet another week passes, and the man returns with a million dollars to give the monk. He places the money at the monk's feet and again asks for the monk to teach him.

The monk looks at the man and asks him, "Is this money for me?"

The man replies, "Yes," then tells him to take the money to share his learnings.

The monk takes the money and throws it on the blazing fire in the hearth.

The man shouts, "What do you think you're doing?"

The monk smiles at the man and says, "That is your lesson, now please be on your way."

This story parallels the truth that money can't buy you happiness or enlightenment, no matter how many "teachers" and gurus out there tell you otherwise. Money can make your life more comfortable. It can afford you freedom and choices. It can also allow you to help others, engage in philanthropy, and be more charitable. But it doesn't guarantee happiness or quell the searching inside unless your money-making activities are accompanied by sincere inner work. Money earned alongside right living, in alignment and guided by your inner wisdom, can be a wonderful, positive experience, as can any aspect of life when you choose to live from your Truth, guided by your Soul.

Many revere Jim Carey as an icon of success and wealth. His story represents many stories of humble beginnings, the struggle to get ahead, and ultimately the power we all hold to overcome and achieve great outer success. But the real beauty of his story is that his success, money, and fame didn't bring him happiness or fulfillment he expected they would. He's very open about this fact. He quit high school at the age of fifteen to help support his family after they lost everything and were living out of a van. He went on to attain an iconic level of wealth and celebrity. He then discovered that success alone, without spiritual work and sitting comfortably with his own shadow, did not lead to fulfillment. That's when he began his spiritual work in earnest. He says, "I think everyone should get rich and famous and do everything they ever dreamed of so they can see that it is not the answer."

At the age of thirty-eight I was finally shown the path to my own spiritual unfolding, although it was almost instantly convoluted by the idea that the path was about having success and wealth. The insidious idea was that I would be rewarded for going through my dark night of the soul and once I became a spiritual person, every whim and desire would manifest itself instantly. How "icky" to think we should automatically be rewarded for doing the work we came here to do. How entitled. It's this entitled attitude that's harming our planet, depleting our resources, and ultimately leading to our own destruction.

This endless quest for wealth, notoriety, and materialism fed my unconscious ego. It was like a hamster wheel; no matter how fast I ran, I was never fully satisfied, but I was always exhausted. The deeper I went into the dream of creating riches and success, the more disconnected and unauthentic I felt. I was living on credit cards, traveling, and buying things I couldn't afford. I was living a fallacy, all in an effort to make people think I had made something of myself. I was projecting the image of someone successful so people would like me; so maybe, eventually, I would like myself! I was so worried about what others thought of me, I was completely delusional to the truth of where I really was. I was living a lie, and the worst manipulation of all was how I would twist things around so I could believe this life was my truth. This disconnection from Self left me feeling extremely lonely. It led to more consumerism and materialism (to try to fill the void and squash my gnawing feelings of shame and worthlessness), which in turn led to more guilt about the excessive spending. Then I would spend even more to try to escape those "bad" feelings. The cycle was endless, feeding into addictive tendencies and eventually leading to depression. All the while my soul was knocking on the door of my consciousness. Eventually, the knocking became too loud to ignore.

We resist hearing the message that money won't bring happiness. But the truth is, it doesn't matter what you achieve on the outside if you're not attending to what's on the inside. Who you are on the inside; the truths, the lies, the things you feel you must hide - they're still with you no matter how much you earn. But, so is the deep yearning that calls to your soul. The dissonance intricately patterned into our belief system makes us believe it will be different for us. Meaning we secretly think, "I am not like everyone else, and when I have money I will feel accepted and it will make me happy."

Realizing money will not make us happy is a hard thing to accept after a lifetime of having "shiny success" shoved in our faces and held up as the ultimate goal. Glossy magazines and television ads show shiny, happy people. The idea that *having more will lead to happiness* silently permeates our society and our consciousness. Our unacknowledged feelings, unresolved needs, traumas, and deep inner-child wounds need attention, and "more money" will never solve these inner conflicts. Many of us believe we don't have the right to have a voice, to express ourselves, and be heard if we don't have money. Having "things" may temporarily give us a false sense of worth; however, if our value is tied to ever-changing outside circumstances, we're in trouble. When we are in a constant state of need (needing more, needing things to be different, etc.) we exist in a perpetual state of "not enough" and we seek *even more* to try to fill the hole that's inside. Our need is a ravenous machine that's never satisfied. We live in a world that caters to that unhealthy idea and capitalizing on it, so companies can sell more stuff and corporations can make more money. With this view of life, no matter how much we make and how much we consume, we will always need more.

Our need for great wealth is a seed that was planted in our DNA at the time of Sumerian civilization. With the creation of the first known organized law came the exchange of currency and debt. We live in a culture today that emphasizes the idea that we are meant to have abundance and all that we desire. "It's our birthright," say the gurus and law of attraction teachers. Somehow, in the new age, this belief has become tied into being spiritual! We're taught we can "manifest" whatever we want with no real connection to what our Souls really need. I know this story very well. I fell into this new-age trap and felt I should have all I desired simply because *I deserved it,* and even better, God wanted me to have it! People buy into the idea that this is the way, the path to enlightenment. We may even feel superior to others because we feel we have found the way, while they remain in the dark.

Throughout this chapter, you may have formed the impression that I'm suggesting money is somehow inherently bad, not spiritual, or that we shouldn't earn what we need. I have no issue with money. Earning good money makes sense, and to be compensated for your work and the value you bring to the world is a beautiful thing. Money is simply a currency. The point I seek to make is that money itself doesn't bring happiness. Only through the inner work of the Soul do we find happiness and fulfillment. The quest for wealth, fame, and success can be downright harmful. When you have done the sincere work of your soul, you will find you need far less, you have greater fulfillment and different motivations. You can still create external success, but you create from a different place and for a different reason. This type of creation, the one without expectation or entitlement, must come through you because it's your Dharma. Your "purpose" is why you *think* you are here; your Dharma is why you *are actually* here. When we create with the expectation that we will be rewarded, with only the end in mind, the creation is about the ego and is results-driven. When you are creating in your Dharma, joy comes from the creating; the joy is in the process.

The way the world is currently set up, we need money to live. There's no denying that. When parts of us have become more conscious, we find our understanding of money is different. How we need money and how we spend it changes. I often think about what the world would be like if the focus wasn't on the money. What kind of world would we create if we had a different priority? Could we create heaven on earth if the focus wasn't on greed?

●

"If you prefer smoke over fire
then get up now and leave.
For I do not intend to perfume
your mind's clothing
with more sooty knowledge.
No, I have something else in mind.
Today I hold a flame in my left hand
and a sword in my right.
There will be no damage control today.
For One is in a mood
to plunder your riches and
fling you nakedly
into such breathtaking poverty
that all that will be left of you
will be a tendency to shine.
So don't just sit around this flame
choking on your mind.
For this is no campfire song
to mindlessly mantra yourself to sleep with.
Jump now into the space
between thoughts
and exit this dream
before I burn the damn place down.
~ Adyashanti

CHAPTER 3:
THE MONSTER IN THE SHADOWS

"The acceptance of your hate will make you more loving, the acceptance of your weakness will make you stronger, the acceptance of your pain will allow you to be more blissful."

-EVA PIRRAKOS

I was caked in dried blood with a layer of dirt around my nose and mouth. I hardly recognized myself. When I fell to my knees on the side of the mountain, I realized I needed to accept my past choices and embrace the learning of what was happening. Only then would I be able to chart a new direction.

Dropping my compass and my coins had been the push I needed to be honest about where I was and to begin discovering my own personal truth. I felt tremendous guilt and shame about not having "made it" to the top of that mountain, about not having found the success I'd been promised was available. I felt so alone. However, in the depths of these feelings, I began to realize that we are each unique, the path for one person will be different from the path for another. I realized I must make my own way and find the place where I belonged.

I continued my slow descent down the rugged hillside into the untouched valley. The valley of shadows. As I was walking, many of the other travelers looked upon me with scorn, as though I was doing something awful. Several told me I was going the wrong way, that their way was the only way to reach the top of the mountain. They told me I would never make it without any tools. I had no money and I no longer carried the compass for guidance. I felt lost but trusted I would find my way. Something within me began to wake - ancient wisdom and knowledge that had been dormant within me and my family for generations. As if we'd been off of our path for hundreds of years. I felt I was bringing healing to myself and my ancestors simply through the choice of trying something different - by trying to make my own way. As I walked, I often felt a loving presence behind me, but when I looked there was no one there. I thought to myself the spirits of my ancestors must be walking with me from within.

I also felt a darker presence. It loomed over me, even in the bright sunshine. There was no escape from it. As I descended further into the valley it only became stronger. A whisper in the wind told me it was time to become familiar with the darkness. When I was off the mountain I could feel the sacredness of the majestic valley of shadows. I knew I was about to face my truest, darkest self.

I was famished, weary, and parched. I looked around the valley for food and water to nourish myself and was immediately reassured. The contrast between the depleted forest on the mountain, filled with hungry travelers, and this bountiful land of game trails, lush green grass, and flowing streams allowed me to appreciate the generosity of our Mother Earth. I followed what I thought was an animal highway, an area where the grasses were flattened, creating a path wide enough for me to walk with ease. It led to a large meadow rich with edible berries and herbs. After I had my fill, I noticed trails going in all directions. Wandering on one of the trails I arrived at a large watering hole and bubbling spring full of fresh, clean water. I dropped to my knees and drank for the first time in a long while. With water dripping down my chin and my hands still immersed in the pool, I caught sight of my reflection. I felt this primal side of me that I'd ignored for many years. I carefully took off my dirty clothes and laid them neatly on a rock. I walked slowly into the river and bathed in the cool, healing waters of the dark valley of shadows.

It felt as though I were bathing in water pumped directly from the veins of the heart of my mountain. As dusk neared I knew I needed to find shelter to sleep and to rest my weary body and mind. I explored the edges of the water and found a thicket of foliage wrapped perfectly into a space large enough for me to crawl into for the night. As I settled I felt completely at ease and comfortable, a feeling of profound safety I hadn't experienced since leaving my mother's womb. I was overcome with a sense of nurturing and I fell into a deep, restful sleep.

In my slumber I dreamed of a large and looming presence in the darkness. At first, I felt afraid. The presence took the form of a shimmering spider. As she descended toward me on a silken thread all my fear melted away. Her message to me was this: "All the things you will be shown are going to test you. They're here to help you develop the courage needed to continue your journey." I breathed deeply. The trepidation I'd been feeling about my departure from the "regular mountain" began to lift. As the spider departed she left me with these words, "Darkness feeds on your ego's desires, but on this path, you will find what you truly need and discover fulfillment."

Suddenly I woke up. A chill in the air had pulled me from sleep. I felt the presence of something big and dark all around me. It brought panic and fear to the core of my being. Everything I'd ever been afraid of was looming over me with seething, yellow eyes and huge pointed teeth. It drooled on me, a black poison dripping from its disgusting mouth. It stared me down, forcing me into submission. I was terrified, cowering, and shivering. I knew was surely going to die. I curled into the fetal position and began to bawl. As my crying lessened I noticed nothing had happened to me. The monster hadn't eaten me and I was still here. I continued to cry for hours until I slipped into a fitful, restless slumber.

I awoke a while later to the sun in my eyes. I looked at the foliage and saw a large spider web adorned with dew glinting in the light. It had not been there the day before. When I crawled from my comfortable nook, I remembered the fear and terror of the night, which I had thought would consume me. I sat waiting for the monster to appear from the bushes and take me, but nothing happened. After a while, I decided it was time to move on. I prepared to make my way to my new mountain, but I still had to traverse the large and dark valley of shadows which loomed ahead of me. As I walked, the landscape changed, growing darker and denser with every turn. The trauma I experienced the night before crept up on me and followed each step I took. Suddenly I was lacking the confidence I had when I started on this new path. What if I'd made a mistake? Surely it would have been safer to stay on the other mountain that everyone else was on.

A wave of deep-rooted anger set in and I felt frustration with every move I made. How could following my heart have turned out this way? Wasn't I supposed to get some sort of positive reward for taking this big step or some kind of affirmation from a higher power? The cool waters and the fresh berries of the meadow were behind me. I was alone and afraid now in this large, dark valley. I couldn't help but doubt my decision. Looking over my shoulder, I realized I was deep in the valley and I couldn't find my way back even if I wanted to. I was past the point of no return. The only option was to keep moving forward, placing one foot in front of the other, carrying my doubts, questions, and frustrations with me. My mountain was barely visible above the tree line miles ahead, with the ominous valley of shadows spanning like a dark sea between. With each step, my perturbed feelings brought a new level of sickness to my being, but I could no longer deny my truth. I couldn't pretend anymore. No matter what, I had to go on. A sudden gust of wind passed carried a message, "Get out of your head and be present to what is happening around you. You will be okay."

●

There's a part of the ego that prevents us from knowing our true Selves. This part can be referred to as "the monster in the shadows." It's the unconscious part of who we are and how we interact with the world. Often we don't realize the unconscious parts of ourselves are holding us back and keeping us in patterns that are detrimental to our existence. Lurking inside each of us, our shadow Self hides and distorts our truth. As we walk through life our shadow is constantly with us, but we do not pay attention to the darkness that follows us everywhere. We lack the awareness to see and understand the darkest and most insidious parts of our ego. These are the parts that drive our never-ending need for *more* and *better*. We'll never be satisfied with what we have as long as this unconscious shadow continues to feed gluttonously on our unquestioned and false desires. Many spiritual teachings suggest the ego must die, that we must completely surrender our identities and that which differentiates us from others, to eliminate our suffering. This isn't true; we need to shine a light on our egos and bring all parts of them to our conscious awareness. My friend Bernhard Guenther says, "We need the ego to live in the third dimension. It isn't about killing the ego, it is about bringing the ego conscious."

When we can bring healing to our shadow, we need less and we develop a clear definition of what brings us fulfillment. Then we are able to sit comfortably with our Truth and the authenticity of our feelings, even the "negative" ones. We are not perfect beings, and that's what makes each of us perfectly unique. Allowing ourselves to be accepted, naked, and vulnerable, just as we are, is the truth that allows us to tap into our innermost being. The ability to own our feelings of being irrational, wrong, needy, defenseless, and unhappy is the key that unlocks our potential for acceptance, independence, and fulfillment. I believe that how we treat ourselves and others in times of deep despair, loneliness and shame are our true measurement for success.

When we're able to step back and observe the work that's being given to us in our darkness, it is clear that the monster lurking in our shadow is there to support our Soul's evolution. It's only when we stop fearing the monster and see that our fear itself is what fuels it and allows it to constantly feed on us that we can break the cycle. We live in a society that perpetuates the concept that negative feelings are wrong and that we can bypass them altogether, "changing state" and transmuting them into the positive feelings that we wish to feel. The problem with this is we're missing out on the lessons wrapped up in the emotions. Within our pain and discomfort is precious information waiting to be acknowledged and absorbed. But in order to release their gifts of wisdom, emotions need to be felt and released, not stuffed down.

You are a pool of water, and your emotional experiences are like mud dredged up from the murky bottom. You have to wait for it to settle before the water unclouds. Give yourself time to become clear. Sink into your fear and allow your darkness in; give yourself time and patience. It is a delicate process allowing the uncomfortable parts of you to just *be*, and allowing those negative emotions to be felt. To begin, simply observe their existence. Then cherish and nourish them. Once you've sat with yourself and your emotions long enough, you begin to release all the false ideas and ego-generated images you have of yourself. You begin to take off layers and remove masks. Learn from them, listen, and pay attention to what you will uncover.

At a certain point in my life, I suffered from suicidal tendencies, which I spent a lifetime trying to evade. Little did I know those intense emotions and experiences were attempting to bring me the most important lessons of my life. It wasn't until I was able to sit with the feelings and listen without resisting that I was able to understand what they were trying to tell me. In these whispers of Truth was potent information which needed to be heard without judgment. The Truth surprised me! I realized I didn't want to die. I was experiencing emotions so deep and intense that I didn't know how to be with them, and I didn't know how to live.

As I became accustomed to simply sitting with my emotions, I noticed they all had something to teach me, and I only suffered when I tried to outrun them or distract myself from them. For example, before I learned to sit with my loneliness, it caused me to act out with self-sabotaging behaviors. I would reach out to people and situations that weren't in my best interest. Until I was willing to sit with these feelings and not take any action, I wasn't able to hear what was being communicated to me. After listening, I was able to find healing and connect to that deep well of divine wisdom that bubbles from within. If you can't just sit in your shit, you will always have to numb it.

For the seeker who is truly looking to shed all untruths, there's a natural ebb and flow to the cycles of expansion. The cycles tend to move us through stages of limbo, chaos, and ease. The burden we're trying not to feel must be understood; it is relevant to our path. The secret to embracing the burden is patience and kindness. This leads to a new awareness that helps you move past the challenge; unless of course, you ignore the opportunity for the lesson, in which case you are simply choosing to repeat it at a later date. All of our emotions offer incredible learning, and they will all come back to us if we don't learn them the first time. Pleasure, pain, and everything in between. There's information in all of it. Trying to live in a prolonged state consisting only of happiness has us missing out on the deep and varied experience of life, which the full spectrum of emotions brings. The way back home to your Self is to feel. You must feel to heal. Unprocessed, ignored, and bypassed feelings turn into discomfort and disease. Suppressed feelings hold you back from your true potential. Vulnerability is the only answer here. Our need to quickly find a solution prevents us from sitting in the understanding that comes with vulnerability, compassion, and empathy. The past can control us and predict the future if we do not find acceptance with who we are and where we have been.

So often in today's world, we are distracted and not present. The most powerful knowledge we can offer in this day and age is to get out of your head and be present to what's happening around you and is being given to you. When you have tunnel vision that focuses solely on your goals, it eliminates the possibility of experiencing the Mystery of Life, which is happening all around you every moment. This moment needs you to open your eyes. The pieces of information waiting for you in the present require your full attention. They are needed to prepare you to move gracefully into the next moment. If you are changing your state and trying to be in a constant state of growth, you are in your head. Whereas when you are present, you can be the observer. Only then will the knowledge and wisdom come forward.

I found freedom walking down the street I grew up on. The intense reality of my previous decisions was weighing heavily on me. I dropped to my knees and allowed myself to feel the burdens of my past. The intensity of the feelings was so overwhelming, I had to surrender to allow them to move through me. It felt as though my entire being was on fire, alchemizing everything I'd previously held as true. This acceptance offered a portal for me to find rebirth. I was able to understand that the feelings were needed to bring healing to the part of my shadow that had plagued me for so long. After hitting rock bottom and later trying to find acceptance of the addictive tendencies which had defined my past, I realized this part of my story would own me until I accepted and embraced it fully. I would never be free to create a different life for myself if I tried to keep it hidden. I could have chosen to hold onto it as my identity; instead, I chose to let it be an experience that moved through me, teaching me valuable lessons about how I choose to live in the present, which now shapes my future.

Each moment we choose to fully experience has information which requires our attention. It's important information we need in order to take our next step. We are required to be fully conscious and embodied. If we are changing our state or trying to remain in a constant state of happiness or continuous productivity, we're not present; again, we are in our heads. When we can be present and be the observer, wisdom and knowledge come forward. The trials and tribulations in our lives are exactly what the Soul needs to evolve. Stop trying to bypass them.

I realize now that only I have the ability to decide how many times I will make the same mistakes and choices. Learning how to sit in the discomfort allows us to expand. In that expansion is where we have the ability to make different choices and grow. It's interesting to discover that all we've been running from (the monster in the shadows) is, in fact, our best teacher. The parts of ourselves we have been ashamed to acknowledge and allow ourselves to express can become our greatest allies. We ashamed to express our true nature, and we are afraid to show others who we really are because we believe we are somehow bad. Are we so afraid that those "ugly" parts of ourselves are so unlovable that we will never be accepted?

CHAPTER 4:
THE NAKED TRUTH

"I am not what I think I am, and
I am not what you think I am.
I am what I think you think I am."

- CHARLES HORTON COOLEY

A rush of wind containing wise words from Spirit washed over me: "When you embrace your shadow parts and express your Truth, you will be free." I heard this and was enraged. How am I supposed to feel all that is inside of me? What about what I want? My feelings of entitlement and victimhood reared their heads. My inner five-year-old self threw me on the ground in a massive temper tantrum. I screamed, "I don't know how to do this! I just want the answers!" As I lay in the dirt feeling wretched, I hated myself and my life. "You are worthless and a failure," I said to myself. This brought a tidal wave of emotions; grief, sadness, terror. Was I going to die out here in this valley? Basking in my feelings of stupidity and helplessness, I grew even angrier with myself. Why did I leave the path that everyone else was on? In that moment, I did want to die. I'd had no idea the journey would be this hard, and I was questioning if it was even worth it. I didn't want to feel this. I was pushing it away and resisting it, which was making it even worse.

As I lay there drowning deep in the mud of my emotions, I heard a whisper through the trees, "Breathe and relax your body." I took a big breath and let it out, followed by another. I began to release all the tension in my body, letting it drain into the ground. Slowly I noticed the intensity of the feelings was subsiding. I began to come around. I pulled myself up and rested on my knees. I noticed my body was hungry, thirsty, and tired. My stomach wanted food. The mountain I'd left behind had plenty of food. In fact, they'd been clearing the forests to create more space to grow crops and raise cattle. The berries I'd eaten a few days ago seemed like a feast! Then a little voice deep inside of me reminded me I must keep going. I got up and stumbled on.

As I walked, the terrain became less forgiving - rocky, and hard to navigate. I slipped and twisted my ankles often. I was losing my confidence and my pace slowed to a crawl. As I moved, I felt a sharp, piercing pain in my left calf. I whipped around to see a large snake slithering away without a care in the world, almost as if it had bitten me for pleasure. This sent me into a state of complete hysteria. My vision began to blur and panic set in. I called for help, but there was no one around. Moments later, I found an outcrop of rocks that was like a small cave. I pulled myself under it to take shelter.

As I faded in and out of consciousness, I prayed that death would take me; it was unbearable. I was quick to give up and thought I'd misjudged my own ability by taking this path. I'd wanted to find my own mountain, but the quest to do so had defeated me. I had no chemicals with me to numb the pain, and I slammed my fists in agony. In my hysteria, I began to hallucinate. I met many beings I did not recognize, but I could feel their presence all the same. Some were there to inhabit my soul and others came with information to guide me. This was when the beautiful, shimmering spider reappeared, weaving her precious web to keep me safe. In this web of creation was my Dharma. The spider left me wrapped in her web, and although it provided some protection, the pervasive darkness was still all around threatening to creep in and inhabit my soul. It wanted to keep me in a state of paralyzed fear. It was foul-smelling and all-encompassing. It began to seep through the web; both physical and ethereal, it consumed everything around me and within me. It stole the breath from my lungs. I felt as though it was trying to take my heart out of my chest. I felt as though I had nowhere to turn, nowhere to run, and nowhere to hide. I had never felt anything even remotely like this when I was living numbed-out in the village; any fleeting moment of pain or discomfort was instantly masked, covered up, or washed out altogether. I never allowed myself to fully succumb to this darkness, and now it felt like it would eat me alive.

In this moment, I was innately present to the truth of what I'd been running from my entire life. I'd been running from my own Truth and who I needed to become to live it. I was running from the feelings that were needed in order to remember myself. I had no idea that from this place of agony and darkness, I would find me. In this naked Truth, as I began to face my own darkness there in the valley of shadows, I would finally begin to find freedom through acceptance.

●

We all wear masks in order to portray to the world what we think is acceptable, and what we believe people need to see in order to love us. We hide behind our masks and we spend a lot of energy pretending that our truth is something other than what's real. We stuff our Truth, cover it up, numb it out, and go on with the charade that we are something else; living a different life behind closed doors as opposed to what we show publicly. Yet, we're unhappy because we are not living what is true for our experience. We may not be living in alignment with our uniqueness, because the truth of our individuality may cause others to cast judgment upon us. It's a process to step into who we really are. It takes work and sincere humility to be able to offer our true expression of ourselves to the world. It's a state of consciousness that must be achieved by being willing to feel and face the undesirable within. In this discomfort is our growth.

When we don't have a strong sense of our own true identity, we tend to craft an ego-based version from our personal wants and desires. But finding long-lasting fulfillment only comes from knowing yourself. When you base your life exclusively on wants and desires, it will always trump fulfillment. You will search endlessly outside of yourself for something to fulfill your desires (and fill the hole inside). External fulfillment is fleeting and without the internal fulfillment gained through knowing yourself and living your

Truth, you'll find yourself trapped in an endless cycle of consumption, wanting, and needing more. The very act of wanting is denying our true emotional state; because the Truth is, we already are all that we're seeking. When you do not *want* anything, you realize how complete you really are.

There's a difference between genuine needs, and being needy or wanting something. For example, a baby needs nurturing, but a spoiled child becomes needy of attention and learns to want. When we can sit in our feelings of "needing" and "wanting" and stop addressing the symptoms of it (discomfort, feeling anxious, endless seeking, wishing things were different, complaining. etc.), we can see the root cause. For many people who feel they cannot feed their feelings of needing and wanting, it creates a state of perpetual fear and angst. This is similar to people with addictive tendencies.

Addictive tendencies are a symptom of trauma; but in our society, we emphasize treating the symptoms rather than the cause. When someone is traumatized and they haven't developed the tools to deal with that trauma and the painful feelings it brings, they will develop those addictive tendencies to numb the pain to try and cope. We try to treat the addiction (the symptom) rather than the trauma (the cause). This is ineffective and that's why addictive tendencies are so rife in our society today. When we can sit with the Truth of what we're feeling, even extreme emotional pain, and simply allow it to be, we connect to what is real and we're given the opportunity of the lesson held within the discomfort. On the other side of fear is freedom. On the other side of pain is joy. All the learning and the wisdom in the middle of the fear and pain is the essential piece we miss out on if we choose to numb or distract ourselves. It isn't about choosing love or fear. It is loving ourselves through the fear. When we stop wanting to be elsewhere, to have arrived "there," or to be further along in our journey than we really are, we begin to understand the journey is more valuable than the destination. The gold is not in the knowing, the achieving, or the arriving, but in the act of figuring it out and who we become in the process. This is the process of waking up and of remembering who we are.

You may have noticed I use the phrase "addictive tendencies" instead of saying addictions. This is because I don't believe in addictions in the way we normally describe them; I believe we are prone to have tendencies that help us deal, manage, and numb pain, trauma, and suffering. Addictive tendencies arise when we have emotions we've never been taught to process. We all have trauma in our past, even if it seems comparatively small. It's the trauma that leads to the tendencies, and in sitting with the trauma we find healing. Society treats the addiction (which is just a symptom), not the wound underneath.

It isn't about creating an avatar of who you want to be and what you want to show the world, it's about learning to be okay with who you are right now in the rawest sense. It's about loving who you are when you're naked in all of your truth, exposed for the world to see. It is allowing yourself to be present with it without justifying or making excuses for it. It's learning how to be here with yourself and finding acceptance. This level of radical acceptance sets you free. From here you become your "True Self." What is waiting beyond the mind patterns and current thoughts is a version of you that is beyond your wildest dreams. You are more powerful than you can imagine and when you accept yourself like this, and you begin to tap into your unlimited potential. None of this means you can't aim to improve on certain things, but your transformation now comes from a place of acceptance rather than needing and wanting. Now it becomes a flowing experience instead of trying to push a boulder up a hill. Now you move through your emotions instead of becoming stuck in them. Now you can pass through suffering, and you no longer experience the pain and loneliness that comes from hiding behind masks.

The paradox is that the awakening of our truest potential can, at first, be the very thing that keeps us paralyzed. When we know our true nature, when we discover our Truth and choose to express it out there in the world, we perceive that we become completely vulnerable. But in this vulnerability we find our own radical acceptance, no longer needing or waiting for others to accept us, and we are finally able to see ourselves clearly. Stepping into our Truth is the practice of our lives. It's a decision we make in every breath and at every moment, over and over again.

Shedding what is not true for us, taking off our masks and choosing to show our real Selves can feel like standing naked for the whole world to see. It is the complete letting go of the masks that we've used to hide our imperfections and scars for most of our lives. Once the hairy mole on the chin is exposed, there's no unseeing it. We're left with feeling the friction inside that comes from standing with our hairy mole exposed. We think feeling the friction will destroy us, but it's actually the place where expansion waits. How we talk to and about ourselves in this moment shows us where we are on the path to radical acceptance and self-love. If we have self-loathing and are critical of ourselves, we project that onto others, showing them how to feel about us and how to treat us. It becomes a self-fulfilling prophecy. Instead, if we can own our unique beauty and stand in our own power, then we no longer need to understand what other people feel about us, nor care what they think of us. In this way, we stop giving our power away! But no one can do it for us. Only you can build this muscle and develop this strength inside. Only you can cultivate a satisfying relationship with yourself and the world. Come to think of it - only you know what your orgasm feels like, only you experience your own overwhelming nausea or pain, and only you know what it feels like when you have to poop. Only you and you alone can discern what is right for you and what is true for you. In this ability, you find your unlimited power.

Our ability to be true to ourselves and express our Truth honestly, with every word and action, measures where we are with our level of authenticity. The white lie is one of the most detrimental things on the planet. It breeds a level of disconnection from our actions and our truths. When I tell you I'm late due to traffic, as opposed to telling you the truth - which is I was being lazy and didn't really prioritize being on time - the truth is evaded. The opportunity for growth for both of us is missed. The Truth contains information which is missed when I choose the white lie. The corresponding feelings that need to be felt in the discomfort of speaking the Truth are then avoided. When we are in Truth, we are present to all that is. There's a whole different reality available that we only become aware of when we live in Truth and authenticity. We gain access to a real-time level of consciousness we don't normally have access to when we are lying (or living a lie). The feelings and truth that come with being honest give us access to a deeper level of Self. When we're able to find this level of Truth and acceptance within ourselves, we also experience peace. We understand others are not responsible for our feelings, and especially our happiness.

How we learn to give and receive feedback on our Truth is a game-changer. I call this "the flick." The flick gives us the chance to see the unconscious parts of ourselves and how we show up and respond to them, as well as how we are triggered when sharing the Truth and how we feel when we are receiving. This indicates where we are in our understanding of ourselves. The flick has the ability to sting just enough to support a long-lasting shift. It also supports us in how we share our Truth with others, which can support their evolution and our own. Again, it is embracing the discomfort of things and being willing to share of ourselves, even when it isn't all light and rainbows.

Mark Yegge says, "Every decision has maintenance and consequences." Put another way, living authentically requires awareness of the maintenance and consequences of our decisions. Guilt and shame are so telling. When we're able to play out a scenario before it happens to determine if it is an experience we want to have, then we make a decision based on our highest good, or we choose to repeat the lesson. There is beauty in our shame. It holds the keys to a new level of freedom. It has the potential to change our lives. When we own and embrace our shame, we are free to learn the lessons it holds and make different choices in the present. This is how we evolve. Our emotional response is telling of where we are when we are being given cues and learning from the Universe. Often, in the beginning, our ego is hurt or we feel ashamed when events occur that trigger us. Our pride means we don't like to feel that we're not perfect, but in this Truth lay the keys to our expansion.

For my entire life, I was considered to be overly emotional. I always needed time to deal with pains and disappointments. It was as if my Soul was shattered each time my feelings were hurt or my heart was broken. What I didn't know until much later was that within the depths of my feelings were some of my most sacred gifts. My ability to experience such deep emotional pain and discomfort gave me the ability to have an incredible connection to others' pain. Additionally, I could feel things other people couldn't feel. It was as if my antenna picked up more frequencies than that of people around me. Transmitted on these frequencies was precious information. Once I understood this, I had to learn how to work with it. Learning to receive "the flick" was one of the most challenging parts of my work and one of the most rewarding. All of the parts of my unhealed self or unconscious ego were instantly triggered. Initially, before I learned how to sit with the flick, I went into deep internal dialogue and brutalized myself. I treated myself worse in these times than any other person would have done. Can you relate to this? How do you talk to or about yourself when you feel sick or ashamed?

I quickly learned that how I treated myself when I felt bad was directly connected to the level of Self-work I'd done and my own levels of Self-worth at the time. How I chose to soothe and support myself directly affected how well I received the flick, and how I was able to flow through the emotions. During these times I began to understand that all I'd been seeking from others (love, attention, care, comfort) was actually what I needed to give to myself. My expectation that I must receive this from others was misguided when I looked for it externally. Initially, I didn't know how to offer support to myself in these times; but when I figured it out, everything changed. Learning to observe our own patterns takes an incredible amount of Self-love and compassion. To be able to sit with the Truth of who we have been and allow the process of acceptance to occur requires internal strength, which can be built up gradually like a muscle. Learning how to hold space for ourselves is one of the most magnificently profound and uncomfortable parts of our evolution. To sit in ourselves and observe the emotional response to Truth; our natural response is to want to change or numb what's uncomfortable. The uncomfortable feelings are most often what drives us to numb with food, alcohol, drugs, sex, porn, shopping, etc. We resist the discomfort because we've been taught to avoid it at all costs, and instead manufacture a state that is more acceptably comfortable or how we *want* to feel instead. Choosing to numb or distract ourselves will never offer the expansion into consciousness that we're capable of. It is the ultimate spiritual bypass. Sinking into feelings can be as terrifying as a snake bite, but it won't kill you in that cave. In fact, it offers profound wisdom and is the path to experiencing peace.

The programming of our current society has disempowered us by encouraging us to avoid discomfort and pain. The "positive vibes only" movement isn't helping any longer in our evolution. Learning that we can change our state, and having the tools to do this, can be a useful beginning step in our spiritual journey. However, just because we have the ability to do something doesn't mean we should always do it. Life is cyclical; summer and winter, night and day, high tide and low tide and back to high tide again. We see this evident in nature, yet somehow we've come to believe that if we're not growing, we're dying. Sometimes it's appropriate to "die" in order for new life to be born. The leaves on the trees do it every year. We've become so afraid of any downward cycles in our lives, we are unbalanced. Maintaining a false positive state of being all the time is like being on a sugar high all the time; it's artificial, unhealthy, and exhausting! Those in a perpetual state of growth, with no connection to their Self and their Truth, can be deeply destructive to the world around them. To see this in action, just look at how many corporations operate purely for profit, and how harmful a profit motive is when it's not balanced with an ethical perspective. Uncontrolled growth without wisdom, learning, and cooperation is what cancer cells do! We were never meant to feel happy 100% of the time. We aren't supposed to be motivated and successful 100% of the time either. We weren't meant to always win. Life has ups and downs, cycles, times of growth, and times of shrinking or going inwards. Simply forcing a positive state of being (before taking the time to be with our feelings) can be harmful.

When we live in Truth, we understand that happiness is not an achieved permanent state; it is simply an emotion to be experienced like all others. Happiness is a state of impermanence. It offers an experience, no different from grief or sorrow. Being alive gives us the ability to feel all the hues of emotion. Thinking we are meant to live in one desired emotion is denying the evolution of our potential. Of course, choosing to sit with and feel the pain is different than taking up residence there. Often when you find yourself in the depths of despair and you're stuck there, it's because you're resisting the very emotions you need to feel. Once you allow them, you will flow through the experience and it will naturally change again. This is life; up and down. Your job is to learn to ride it. What's interesting is that when you learn to be with all of your emotions, you may not be as affected by them. The rollercoaster becomes a gentler ride. However, if you've spent a lifetime resisting your pain, you may need to be willing to spend a little longer "down there."

Often people feel it's their job to cheer others up. It's as though because they attended a seminar or took a course on the power of positivity, they now perceive it as their role to enforce positivity on those around them. While the intention is good, in some circumstances the outcome can be more harmful than helpful. It can be uncomfortable to sit with those who are suffering; if you've ever had someone try to cheer you up when you've been in genuine emotional pain, you know how awful it feels. Often when people are experiencing painful emotions, they need you to hold the space, sit with them, and listen. Don't try to *change* how they are feeling. They will come out of it when they're ready. There are lessons to be learned from the people who cause us the most friction, and often they are our greatest teachers. If we're with people who only believe what we believe, it eliminates the potential for what we could learn from different beliefs. I don't think that we should cut people out of our lives because we deem them as negative; however, if a person is causing you significant harm and trauma, then creating the proper boundary to protect yourself is needed.

At some point in our personal spiritual evolution, we may have learned how to change our state. We may have been taught that there's no need to feel low, to experience depression, or to sit with anxiety. During this part of our journey, we may have adopted a belief that we're somehow superior to those who can't or don't change their state, and we find ourselves feeling that somehow our new-found frequency is going to be impacted by their negativity. This is "new age programming" and is creating an incredible disconnect from what's true and real. It takes away the ability to hold space for each other. You can't take a suffering person into an elevated state and expect they will be able to remain there for any duration. It is a fake state, and it is lying to the Soul and denying what is true. No long-lasting results will remain. If someone is able to hold the changed or elevated state for any length of time, the trauma remains in the body and turns into disease. However, if they had been able to sit with their trauma as it arose, to feel and process what needed to be felt and processed, they would have moved through the trauma, releasing it from the body and moving naturally on to a different state of being. There's incredible learning in every step of the process of actualizing our true state and allowing the alchemical process of feeling to offer a true embodied state of enlightenment. When we allow the ego to tell us we should be feeling something different than what we are feeling, we're forcing a desired state. The same holds true for affirmations. Affirmations are lies we tell ourselves in a bid to convince ourselves we are something we're not. This demonstrates the unconscious ego's need to try and force an outcome. It highlights the parts of ourselves we have not yet begun to work on, the parts which are still in the shadows.

I remember the first time I was consciously able to be "in" someone else's experience. At first, it was brutal. I felt their physical discomfort and understood on some level their emotional pain. I felt incredible pressure in my stomach and chest. But I found I was able to sit with them, even though I felt sick and wanted to retreat. In that moment, I was able to hold the space they needed in order to be vulnerable and feel safe. Although I understood it helped them, I couldn't handle how it affected me. Maybe I had always felt the pain of others to some extent and that's why I'd spent so much of my life feeling anxiety and depression. Some people feel the pain of life more than others and are deeply connected to the suffering we don't see or know is there. When you feel as though you're drowning in the depths of your soul, and you don't understand what's happening there, you can't help but drown the people trying to help you. Not surprisingly, it can be a level of reality others want no part of. This was certainly the case for me. My pain was so deep, it made me weird, challenging to be around, and at times needy, especially in close personal relationships. Until I understood and embraced it, that is. I'm still weird today, and I certainly still challenge people to grow, but I no longer view myself as needy. Rather, at times I have needs which I know I can fulfill myself.

The story of my life was one of suffocating in my emotions and not being able to find the words to express how I was feeling. It was challenging to understand that the only solution was to surrender to the feelings, allowing them to swallow me whole. Learning to sink into my emotions was like sinking into a pot of boiling mud. Gaining the understanding that as the mud took away my last breath, I would break through the ceiling of my feelings and be met with my Truth. Here in this dark place, my naked Truth was waiting for me. As I began sitting with the parts of myself I'd spent a lifetime running from, it felt like hot flashes of my own reality, or like fire; the flames licking my very being, waiting to alchemize all that I'd been avoiding. I finally understood that feeling the Truth isn't as hard or scary as I'd imagined. And in that moment, all that was required was that

I surrendered to it, allowing myself to finally be exactly as I was with no judgment. From this place, my authentic Self was remembered. It was the first step of an infinite number of steps on the journey back to me.

Self-manipulation dirties the lens of who and what we think we are, making it hard for us to see ourselves. For me, one of the most interesting parts was understanding what I was not. I was not the clothes that I wore, the car I drove, or the places I'd been to. I spent a lifetime immersing myself in these material items, trying to figure out who I was. The shadow self needed these labels to find an identity. But now, better questions began to come to mind. Who was I without all the stuff? Who was I in my naked Truth? This process started from the deepest parts of my soul; by accepting the parts of myself that I usually did my best to hide, and by looking directly at myself. I discovered I didn't have a lot going on underneath the labels. I'd spent so much time caring about my designer jeans or bag, I didn't know a lot about my character! I was a good person but had a vein of materialism that ran so deep it infiltrated every part of me. I had been living my life to buy stuff. I lacked the ability to find presence and beauty in anything that was simple or to connect with the breath of life because I was so focused on achieving this desired state and appearing to live a luxurious life.

I realized I was never really content, even in the moments I had all the things I thought I wanted. I always had this feeling I needed to be somewhere else or that something was missing. This endless need to keep seeking was the distraction that kept me from finding the very thing I was looking for! What a crazy trap of the ego. The realization that my Soul had been waiting for me to choose it the entire time was sobering. As this realization washed over me, my body relaxed. I yearned for the love I'd been searching for outside of myself, except now I knew I was the source of that love! All along I'd wanted me to love myself, the way I'd asked others to love me. Isn't that crazy? No one loves the way I love, and I needed to love myself.

In this moment of deep Truth, I opened my heart to Love. A flooding dose of oxytocin enveloped my entire being and for the first time in my life (that I was conscious of), I felt the love I'd been searching for. In that moment my connection to Spirit blanketed me and I felt warm, safe, and renewed. Briefly, I rested in the nirvana of my Soul. I had no words to express what I was experiencing, and then just like that, it was gone again.

A fleeting glimmer of what is possible when we sit with our emotions and embrace our own Truth. Then, all the years of programming, trauma, and dysfunction that were living in my cellular memory and the tissues of my body, came rushing back in. I didn't know at the time, but these were the feelings I was going to need to become comfortable with because within them and through them was an expanded version of me, a new life of more authenticity and Truth.

CHAPTER 5:
THE JUNGLE

"I just want to thank the all of it, all of it."

- MURPHY

Lying on the ground in that small cave, writhing in agonizing pain, I still feared my death was near. My body was filled with panic and adrenaline. Every muscle was tense as I tried to manage the terror I was experiencing. I knew it was my Truth and that I needed to stay in it, but I had never done it before. I was scared. I began to cry hysterically and beg for help. The tears helped to release some of the pressure and they were strangely cathartic. As my body began to relax, I had a vision of a beautiful, delicate fawn with bright eyes. She nuzzled me gently. This brought me some comfort. Then I realized she'd come to me with a message. The message was in her eyes; never wavering, never fearful, but full of love and kindness. The look in her eyes reminded me that fear only has the power we give it, through the meaning we ascribe to it. I understood that I gave my fear its meaning and power, so what was the meaning I would choose? What was the lesson? Then it came to me. "Everything you are being given is what you need to evolve. Each thing you face contains the knowledge to continue. You can choose to be afraid and have it paralyze you, or you can use it as the light to guide the next step of your journey. It will require that you feel it to learn."

After drifting in and out of sleep I was awakened by a faint, but deep, sound in the distance. I listened carefully. I felt a slight rumbling in the ground. Whatever was making the sound was literally shaking the ground beneath me. My mouth was dry as cotton wool, and my joints and body ached, but the noise was becoming louder. Finally, I realized it was drumming! The last thing I felt like doing was getting up, but my curiosity and the fact that I needed to find water meant that it was no longer an option to stay sitting. As I rolled onto my side I could feel my swollen leg, where the snake had bitten me. Parts of it were numb and it was a shocking color, a mix of yellow, green, and bluish tinges. *Still, I was alive!*

I dragged myself to my feet only to find I was almost too weak to move, but I remembered my dream and the message from the spider. *I had to keep going, no matter what.* Only I could save myself, or I would die trying. This was the truth. With this new sense of Self-trust awakening, I found strength and took steps towards the sound of the drums. They were coming from deep inside a dense jungle, and I pushed through. As I drew closer, I could hear voices. With every step, my courage was returning. I couldn't make out what the voices were saying, but it filled me with the hope that I may be able to receive help. Despite the courage that was growing inside of me, I knew I needed help. My life was fading. *But I couldn't give up now, I was too close.* I was almost to the source of the sound, but my body was exhausted and I fell. As I began to fade in and out of consciousness, the spider came to me once again. I asked if I was dying. She replied that it depended on how I perceived death. Then she said I must listen, she had something important to tell me. "When you meet those who walk in the shadows of the jungle, you must ask them for the healing vine;" I asked if this healing vine would save my life, but then the vision ended. I lay in the brush unable to move, and once again waited for death. I drifted slowly away.

Suddenly the smell of incense smoke filled my nostrils and I woke in front of a fire. My leg was wrapped and there was a gooey, green substance oozing out of the makeshift bandage. A woman appeared with a pitcher of water and a plate of food. I smiled weakly as she handed me a cup of water. As I gulped the water I felt as though nothing had ever satisfied me so completely. I asked for more and as I drank, I could feel it nourishing every cell of my body. I thanked the woman and asked for her name, but she didn't reply. A gentle half-smile tweaked the edges of her mouth, enough for me to know she acknowledged me. Another woman came over to examine my leg. As she removed the bandage I could see that my leg was completely healed! *How could this be?* I asked her how was this possible, but again I received no reply, only a loving gaze. I was filled with confusion. I clearly hadn't imagined the snake bite, *yet now there was no sign of it.* Perhaps they'd given me the healing vine my spider had mentioned.

As I ate the food she gave me, I noticed my strength coming back. It felt as if it was nourishing not only my body but my entire being. I asked for another plate to keep eating, I didn't want to stop. But the women gestured that it was enough. I lay for several hours on the soft blankets by the fire, and I felt truly safe for the first time. I thought back to the overwhelming feelings of anger, desperation, and fear that had surfaced when I was distressed. I remembered feeling like a victim, and this put me in a state of wanting to give up. *This insight was helpful.* The next time I was in a stressful situation and had feelings of fear and hopelessness, instead of resisting and letting them overtake me, I now had the ability to sit with them, allowing them to be, rather than reacting. I could choose to feel and *observe* my feelings, rather than being overcome by them. There was knowledge waiting for me in that experience. I did not need to run from it or try to refuse it. I had gained the ability to choose whether I wanted to react or observe. I had not mastered it, *but this new awareness was the first step.*

I made another attempt to communicate with the women nearby and asked if they had used the healing vine to heal my leg. They gave each other a knowing look but didn't answer me. I felt confused and wondered what was blocking our ability to communicate. I found myself growing sleepy. I laid back and once more fell into a blissful slumber. While in dreamtime I met an old woman who resembled my Grandmother. She looked at me directly in the eyes. Her wise Soul and comforting presence were like a blanket that swaddles an infant. Her message was strong but simple. "The information you are seeking will only be found in surrender." I awoke as the dusk faded and night drew in. A very pungent smell assaulted my nostrils and I sat up to discern what it was. I found a bubbling pot of dark black mud next to me. The very sight of the mud evoked feelings of angst and fear. I did not know what to expect next, but I guessed this mud was meant for me! As the mud cooled, I was enveloped in a smoke bath of tobacco and what smelled like sage. I felt the women were preparing for something big, but I had no idea what to expect. The women gathered around me forming a circle, in what appeared to be a silent prayer. As I watched them pray, an intention was birthed from the depths of my soul. *I intended to find the tools that would help in my journey to the top of my mountain.* Just then one of the women approached me and gave me an ancient-looking hand-carved wooden cup that was tainted and stained with residue from the past. Inside was a dark liquid.

Medicine. Was this the healing vine? They all looked expectantly at me. As I lifted the cup to my lips and tasted the bitter liquid, my stomach churned. I attempted to pull it away from my mouth, but one of the women firmly pushed it back to my mouth and I drank. I could feel myself salivating in an attempt to help the mud slide down my throat. The intensity of the bitter and earthy flavor of the medicine instantly caused my body to shudder and I almost vomited. I tried to get up to move, but the women pushed me firmly back down. The message was clear; I was supposed to sit with this. I was afraid, but I needed to stay. I had to stop running from it. As the night sky turned black, the stars peeked through a thick canopy of trees. Hundreds of winged creatures I assumed were bats flew over my head, chattering and feasting on the night's bounty. As I listened to the sounds of the night, I had another realization. *It was time to let go of past thought patterns and regrets.* This is what would allow me to sit here now. Once I began this journey into the valley and the unknown, I knew there was no turning back. The desire to beat myself up over my decision was not helpful or necessary. I was there now, as I was supposed to be. I couldn't continue up the old mountain, because it wasn't meant for me. *It never had been.*

Vivid colors and geometric shapes danced before my eyes. Every object I looked at was perceived in a new light. *I saw them in a way I had never seen them before.* As the intensity of the experience overcame me, I felt as though I kept reaching a new level of climax. They scared me, I felt fear with every wave. Reminding myself to breathe, I found the intensity of the experience both profoundly beautiful and terrifying. Like a roller coaster of both fantasy and nightmare. The medicine was taking me through waves of full-on experience, with small moments of time to recover before the next big wave. Like the surf in the sea pounding you under, and then bringing you to the surface for one more breath before the next wave hits. The more I resisted, the deeper the medicine pulled me in. The image of the old woman from my dream floated into my vision. I heard her words but found myself resisting. Fire began to engulf me. I felt my heart racing and I began to shiver with cold sweats. "Welcome to the jungle," I thought. This was the beginning of the next leg of my journey.

●

Many people who are seeking to improve themselves end up gorging on self-help and become caught in the endless pursuit of success, growth, and personal development. However, it's this excessive pursuit that can keep them from reaching their deepest well of internal knowing. The seeking keeps us in a continuous loop of needing more. Comfortably numb or endlessly seeking; neither path is fulfilling, and neither leads to true enlightenment. There's no place in either scenario to simply *be*. Often the answer to our ailments and troubles is the very thing we don't want to do. Nothing: to just be where we are and learn to accept what is, right now.

Many do not choose to hold still in the now, rather they will choose to re-wrap their discomfort into a new pursuit, mission, ailment, drama, or preferred state of chaos. The path to real fulfillment, tapping into the unlimited potential and even enlightenment, requires the ability to make different choices. It requires that one be willing to let go and surrender. Meeting our wounds and burdens with patience and grace, instead of numbing with more goals, achievements, successes, and materialism. The shadow of our deepest Selves is brought forward to examine, understand, accept, and allow the ego to become conscious. It requires us to walk through the darkest part of our Soul and to learn to sit quietly in the shadows. We must willingly enter into our own dark jungle. It is a daily practice, one that will create unimaginable shifts throughout every area of your life.

Let's talk about fear. For most people, the idea of sitting still with fear is so terrifying that the thought alone will prevent them from even considering it. Fear is such a funny thing. So many people have portrayed it as something that isn't real. While I understand why they say this, my own experience with fear has been different. For me it *is* real (just like the other emotions) and I found myself running from it most of my life. But that's the thing - once you start running, it's hard to stop! When I did finally stop and face my fears, I learned something amazing. Fear is my friend. Fear only has the power we give it. Even my deepest and most irrational fears were there to tell me something. If I push them out of my mind, I am missing the opportunity to learn the knowledge they bring. I have developed a method to help me understand and work with my fear. I examine the fear by peeling back the layers to see what's underneath. Then I imagine the worst-case scenario. What would I do if that happened? When I've come up with a solution to the worst possible thing, *I'm no longer afraid.* Once I realized this, I also became aware that I could handle any emotions and anything that happens

The resiliency we discover within ourselves during times of struggle and when we choose to stay conscious is the spark that ignites our courage. Often we're so quick to give up and much of the time it's easier to just quit. But then we miss the learning. The will to carry on is stronger when you have limited choices. Most people in this new age have so many choices and options. Survival is not an issue in western cultures, with modern conveniences and international commerce. We live in a time of instant gratification. Everything we desire is available with the push of a button or waiting at the nearest store, which is usually no more than a few miles away. Unlike our ancestors, we don't have the need to find food and shelter every day or to search for water. We just turn the faucet and clean water magically appears. Yet, despite all of this convenience and wealth, many people feel less spiritually nourished than ever before. We have so much of what we want, but do we have the things we really need? Those things which nourish our Souls. Have we become physically gluttonous at the expense of our well-being?

When we find ourselves in a situation where our Souls feel as though they are dying, we finally start to ask better questions. How do we really nourish the Soul? How do we begin to live in harmony with our home, our Mother Earth? Within these questions is great friction. We are confronted with taking the very action we fear most, in order to change things. Most people avoid friction at all costs. But, not only do we need to go there, we need to be able to sit in the friction. *That's what will set us free.*

There comes a time in our journey when we are ready to understand the parts of ourselves that keep us from the things we are meant to do. The parts of ourselves that have trauma or disconnection, the parts requiring we go into them and *feel* what is needed to release them. We are alive and capable of surfing the waves of the "all of it." The mastery comes in knowing how to sit comfortably in the depths of our darkness.

CHAPTER 6:
THE TRUTH OF LIFE

"Enlightenment is a destructive process. It has nothing to do with becoming better or being happier. Enlightenment is the crumbling away of untruth. It's seeing through the facade of pretense. It's the complete eradication of everything we imagined to be true."

-ADYASHANTI

The medicine was shifting the vivid colors and geometric patterns into stories and experiences. The more I tried to turn away, the more intense the visions became, leaving visceral sensations in my body. Although I was unable to navigate well, I knew what was happening. *I knew what it meant.* The more I tried to run from what I needed to feel, the more intense it becomes. I battled the intense heat and the next minute was overcome by chills as the medicine traveled through the depths of my soul, alchemizing my experiences and the way they were perceived within my being. There was no escaping it. Then I heard a voice talking to me; it was the grandmother from my dream. She asked what I was afraid of. I answered that I wanted to know the Truth, but I didn't want to *feel* all this stuff to know it. Her reply was simple, yet direct, "The fear of feeling is worse than the feeling itself." My fears were keeping me from connecting into my expanded self. My fears kept me blocked from my unlimited truest potential. They weren't meant to be ignored, bypassed, or denied. They were in my life to teach me what I needed to know.

In my vision, Grandmother asked me to lay my fears out on a table. I reluctantly allowed each of my fears to surface, and I put them on the table. She said to look at them carefully and really *see* what they were about. As I looked down, I could see there were five main fears I had been hiding from and running from.

The first was a betrayal of myself. The level of self-manipulation I used to obtain what I wanted kept me distanced from my Truth. I lied to others around me; but even worse, I lied to myself. I didn't care about the consequences of my actions or what they did to my being, *as long as I could have what I wanted.*

Next was my fear of change. I wanted my life to be different so I could have all I desired, but I was disconnected from what I would have to do to make that change, and what I'd have to learn and sacrifice to become that person, I said I wanted to be. I wanted all the benefits, without doing any of the work!

The third fear was a lack of trust in me; the fear that I couldn't take care of myself. I had so much invested in the idea that the answers are found outside of us, I'd lost the connection to my internal guidance system and I'd lost all trust in my Self. I had relied on my family and intimate partners for this sense of trust that I hadn't uncovered in myself.

The fourth fear, which I felt guilt and shame about having, was my need to be seen by others. I was afraid of not being seen, and of not being loved. I'd lied to myself for years, saying I didn't care what others thought, but in reality, I did care. *A lot.*

My fifth and final fear was the fear of dying, or of suffering in death. I lived with the memory of my mother's intense suffering as she was passing from stage four bladder cancer. It was heartbreaking. She was a strong, vibrant, and creative individual. I had always perceived her as unstoppable. Yet cancer stole her strength, aged her skin, and altered her hair from red to grey within days. I had seen that pain changes a person, and although they can find healing, there is a piece they can never get back.

Grandmother looked at me and asked if I understood all the fears and what they were there to teach me. Suddenly my body was overcome with terror; a panic more intense than I had ever experienced before. Calmly, Grandmother took each of the fears off the table and turned them upright, creating a doorway. *She told me all I had to do was walk through it.* For a few moments, I stood frozen, unable to take action or make a decision. She asked me to observe what was stopping me, told me to notice my actions, and asked how often in my life I chose to stay paralyzed in my anticipation of the fear of something, rather than moving forward. My heart was pounding in my ears and I could barely breathe, let alone walk forward. Then I remembered what the spider told me at the beginning of my journey. *That I must continue on, no matter what.* In my vision with Grandmother, I took a slow, deep breath and walked through the doorway of fear, all the while waiting for the surge of pain that would come with all of my feelings hitting me full force. As I crossed over the threshold, intensity like I've never felt before moved through me. I finally surrendered to it and let it overcome me. Once both feet were through the doorway, I found all the fear had dissolved completely. *I couldn't believe it!* Grandmother had said the worst part about the things we fear is the anticipation of feeling them. It turns out she was right. Once we walk through them, they are behind us. A wave of peace surged through me and I felt relief for the first time since the medicine had touched my lips.

Slowly the sensation of peace began to fade and in front of me was an image of a dying planet. Her oceans were polluted and the fish were covered in grotesque tumors. Radiation reached across all corners of the planet. *What struck me most, though, was that the people of the planet were not at the top of the food chain, even though they believed they were!* There was a dark, greedy energy overshadowing the entire planet and all of her beings. This dark force disconnected the people from their homes. Her people cared more about the quest for riches and success than they cared about her. Blinded by greed, which radiated from the dark entity, they were rapidly destroying themselves and their mother planet. I could feel the pain of all the people who were starving to be loved; but just as fast as they loved, love was being sucked out of them by the dark force. *My love alone was not enough to save them.* I could see pigs in cages who were never allowed to stand or stretch their legs. They were fed genetically modified grain and when they wouldn't eat anymore they were force-fed. My vision flashed from the death of these poor creatures to a frying pan in someone's home. The people are gorging on the fried pig meat and feeding it to their children, not realizing the cheap meat from the dying pigs is making them sick. Not realizing the antibiotics (which prevented the pigs from becoming diseased in the squalid living conditions) were being passed on through the meat and assaulting their bodies with disease. Not understanding they were ingesting the fear and suffering of those pigs. The people then started lining up to take pills for their sickness and continued to get sick. More pills, more sickness and disease. I watched an endless cycle of death.

Suddenly I was distracted by the grinding of a giant war machine that was on a path to force new world order. It was surrounded by tanks and soldiers as far as the eye could see. I began to see flashes of bodies throwing themselves from buildings in the cities as the world economy collapsed, people no longer able to feed their families. The food supplies diminished and they were left with only their own skills and resourcefulness. FEMA camps were put in place as a ploy to offer support during these times of collapse. But the FEMA camps became peoples' homes, and the food rations were only offered as long as you agreed to the vaccinations being handed out. Around the perimeter was a barbed wire fence to keep people from leaving.

The panic and terror of the end approaching was so fierce that my body began to convulse. I began to purge. *Then, I heard a whisper from the medicine saying it was time again to surrender.* As I took a breath and lay back on the ground, a gentle voice reminded me that energy cannot be created or destroyed, only transferred. Finally, I surrendered completely. I opened my arms exposing my tender core and allowed my mind to slip into the boiling pot of mud. As I took my last breath, I relaxed my body and allowed myself to feel *everything*. All the fear I'd been pushing away, with it came all the love too. The drums were beating intensely around me and the discomfort of the healing medicine made me want to crawl out of my skin. I fully allowed the experience to envelop me.

As the night grew darker and the fire began to die, I felt a deep chill seeping into my bones. I could still feel the subtle alchemy happening within my mind, body, and Soul. I could still feel the medicine working, still sense her wisdom, feeling it in the smallest wisps of flames and dying embers of the fire. I felt unsettled and shaken, still slightly convulsing from all I'd seen, and yet I felt completely connected to everything. This sacred vine had shown me the way into myself, and I knew that without the medicine I wouldn't have felt what I needed to feel. It helped me to see my ability to walk through my greatest fears. It showed me the Truth I had always known but was too afraid to see until now. I now understood everything I touched must be done with intention and that energy and intention are important. I also now understood I must be fully embodied because there is something greater at hand that requires many of us to walk this path.

When dawn finally broke, taking away the vestiges of a long night, the sun began to shine on my life in a completely new way. The medicine women, who cared for me throughout the night, greeted me with fresh fruit and hot tea. Although no words were exchanged, there was a deep respect and knowledge shared between us. After eating, the women brought me an old gunny sack made of hemp that held food and a flask of clean water for my journey ahead. We said silent goodbyes with our eyes, and our hands held at our hearts. I felt a deep love for these people who held space for me. As I walked away from the clearing in the jungle, everything seemed to glisten and sparkle. I noticed the geometric formation and connectedness of the entire world around me.

With my head full of new understandings and my stomach filled with nourishment, I finally felt I had everything necessary to make it through the valley of the shadows alive. A new light seemed to work its way through the canopy of leaves overhead. This felt good after the darkness I'd experienced previously in my journey. As I pushed through a thicket of foliage, I saw my mountain clearly, growing ever larger as I neared its base. Although I had learned so much already, I sensed my work was just beginning. The night had shifted me and the integration of this new knowledge was the most essential piece that would unfold over the course of my journey ahead.

●

Humans long for experiences; experiences that make us better and happier. From a biological standpoint, the only thing an animal desires is to eat, sleep, drink, and procreate. As sexual beings, our main desire is to produce healthy offspring, but humans have additional, unnatural desires (that we gorge upon) that are destroying our home. So far, we don't care enough to change. We've been programmed to be disconnected from the earth, Spirit, and ourselves. Beyond our own lack of connection, there is something far greater at hand in this destruction.

Bernhard Guenther says that *"everything we see on a global three dimensional level — the ongoing wars, human rights atrocities, oppression, loss of freedom, surveillance, corporate greed, genetic modification, fluoride in the water, geo-engineering, chemtrails, pharmaceuticals, vaccination, religious and political dogma/systems, government, sexual pathologies, racism, mainstream media/entertainment mind control, Trans-humanism/A.I., etc. — is the creation of (or heavily influenced by) occult forces that have been ruling over humanity for thousands of years, using their human puppets to carry out their agenda in classic divide-and-conquer fashion on un-seen levels."*

Once upon a time, everywhere we walked was clean food and water. Our air was safe to breathe, and our greatest dangers were predators and natural catastrophes. Now we face a threat generations before never could have imagined. Environmental destruction that will blindside (if not kill) our children and suffocate their futures. Capitalism has made huge advances in our society at the cost of our home. Globalization has connected us all but also disconnected most of us from the earth and our surroundings. We are missing the point - we are not separate from what is around us! Everything is connected, a holistic system which we are part of, the whole depending on the sum of its parts.

Religion has positioned itself neatly between many people and Spirit. With a true connection to Spirit, the cathedral walls would crumble under the weight of the millennia of fallacies. For most, a building doesn't provide a connection to God. Normally this topic is considered taboo, but the only way for us to be able to connect and turn things around is to start talking about these things. We have to be willing to be vulnerable with our true opinions and experiences - not everyone has the same experience. Our connection to Source, Spirit, God, or Nature is our own and can only be experienced within.

Aside from our disconnection with nature and our Mother Earth, our disconnection to the Self is one of the greatest betrayals of our time, and it shows in how we choose to feed ourselves. We live in a society that is detached from the truth of food and how we choose to nourish ourselves with it. We believe the body is meant to be hacked. "Hacking the body" brings to my mind the image of taking a hatchet and whacking it into what we want it to be, instead of listening to the sacred wisdom that our bodies are communicating to us. In western society, we tend to treat illness of the body and we're not even doing a good job of that at present. Instead, we should be asking, "How can I be well?" Western medicine tends to separate each part of the body, treating each part as though it's separate from the whole. Then we try to treat the symptoms, rather than looking for the root cause of the disease. Here are two definitions of the word "symptom" from an online dictionary:

1. A physical or mental feature which is regarded as indicating a condition of disease.
2. An indication of the existence of something, especially of an undesirable situation.

The symptom is the indication that something is wrong! So why do we behave as if the symptom is the disease itself? In treating the indications of something wrong in our body system, we are effectively putting a gag over our body's ability to communicate with us. Then we wonder why we wind up sick with something serious. An example of our disconnection to what our body is expressing is when a person automatically takes aspirin for a headache, rather than figuring out why the headache is there in the first place. But what about more serious ailments? What about when the symptoms are ongoing - such as regular joint pain, breathlessness, dizziness, extreme fatigue, nausea, constipation, and so on. Our bodies are giving us information all the time. The signals start small, but if we continue to mask them with medication year after year without treating the root cause, our bodies will become sicker until suddenly, out of the blue, cancer, a heart attack, or a stroke occurs. But these things are rarely, truly out of the blue.

Chances are the signs and symptoms were there, but we weren't paying attention. We've given up our power when it comes to our own health. When we have pain, we pop a pill to take the pain away. When we are sick, we look to a doctor or specialist to fix us. We are ostracized by others for feeling the pain when we don't want to take the medication prescribed because our medical system is so brainwashed into believing this is the only way to heal. This isn't to say Western medicine doesn't have a place; it's great for emergencies, surgeries, and diagnosing - but we are missing the fact that we need multiple methods to heal properly. Bringing in different healing modalities from other cultures will help us have a "Whole Approach" to well-being.

Food portions and package sizes are another areas where we've lost control. For example, a bag of chips is not designed for you to eat one or two. They are carefully manufactured with chemicals, flavorings, fat, and salt to ensure you eat the whole bag! And we wonder why we can't stop. Factory farmed meat is not only unethical and inhumanely cruel, but it's full of synthetic hormones, antibiotics, and growth hormones, which causes our endocrine system to be out of whack. It's no surprise that hormonal diseases like endometriosis, PCOS, and "moobs" in men are on the increase at alarming rates. We eat foods that are processed or genetically modified, not realizing the toll glyphosates and other chemicals have on our bodies, as well as on the planet herself. Even when we are aware of the repercussions of these choices, we've created such a cycle of addictive tendencies with food, we don't care that we're drinking something cancer-causing when having a soda or a cheap coffee with syrup. Or, that we're eating diabetes when we open another packet of candy. We think, "I'll get to it tomorrow," until one day there are no tomorrows. We've become so emotionally attached to food that it's hard to break these habits, even with full awareness of the consequences and the best intentions. I have a friend who knows the dangers of aspartame in diet Coke but continues to drink it anyway. (You know who you are, friend. I wrote this for you!) This is where the work is for all of us. We all have habits we need to address in order to reconnect with and honor ourSelves. Often, behind the emotional responses to addressing this work are uncomfortable feelings we'd rather avoid. Once again, we're back to learning to sit with our feelings and being willing to experience the discomfort, rather than using food to numb out.

It's not just food though; we've become gluttonous in many areas of our lives. From the lifestyles we live and the things we buy to the home comforts we take for granted. We've even become greedy with things that are normally healthy for us, such as over-consuming healthy foods, supplements, and other resources. Essential oils are a perfect example of this: it takes sixty roses to make a single drop of rose oil. It takes ten thousand roses to make the five-millimeter bottle of rose oil we buy online. Imagine those ten thousand roses being mowed down for that one little bottle. *It's mind-blowing.* There are more efficient ways to use plants and flowers for healing. At what cost do we receive our coffee beans, our almonds, or our steak? Are we willing to spend more money to pay for organic and high welfare foods? Do we insist on the assurance that our cup of coffee is ethically sourced? Do we care that it was potentially farmed using child slave labor when we're craving that next caffeine fix? These are things we should all consider before our next purchase.

We are living in a worldwide dream full of greed and destruction. Our planet is dying, suffering at the hands of humans with excessive desires, greed, and consumption. *How do we learn to nourish ourselves internally so we can stop the over-consumption?* The degradation of rainforests is sickening. The majority of the destruction of the Amazonian rain forest is caused by creating more pastureland for cattle, not to mention the amount of water each cow needs to drink to end up on your plate. We are living during the time of the greatest mass extinction this planet has seen to date, and we are the root cause of it. This model of capitalism is not sustainable and we must change something before it is too late. However, I fear we may have already reached the point of no return. Capitalists that have fortunes invested in palm oil, beef, and other highly unsustainable agricultural practices couldn't stop if they knew how. They can't stop because the consumers are the true driving force in all of this. We are programmed to eat what we've always eaten, and we've never had the wherewithal to question where our food comes from. Until now!

This isn't intended to make you or anyone feel shame and guilt, as these are not helpful here either. I don't wish to shame anyone for their choices; rather I want to bring awareness to the fact that the cattle industry alone could cause global collapse if things do not change. The rainforests are the earth's lungs, and cattle ranches are a cancer plaguing them. How much money you have, or how beautiful your stuff is, won't matter when there's no more clean air to breathe. We have set ourselves on a course for planetary destruction and we don't even bat an eye. As humans we have five basic needs to survive; food, water, sleep, clean air, and shelter. As we speak, the earth is running out of clean water, our food is poisoned by chemicals, the air is polluted by our industries, our sleep is regimented by our work, and our shelter is threatened by extreme weather. The crux of the problem is over-population and under-caring. Yet we continue to have babies, and we continue with the same old behaviors that caused this mess! My concern is: will there be a planet left for our babies to live on? For much of the planet, having children occurs from an unconscious place. While I understand having a baby can be one of the most amazing experiences, and I respect people's right to have children, we need to think about the consequences of it all.

Gaining an understanding of life at this level also brings a great sense of loss and grief. The way I experienced the world for most of my life was a lie. For a while, this created incredible anger and depression in me. Most people say they want enlightenment, but do not really understand what it is they're asking for, nor do they understand the burdens and responsibilities that come with it. *Enlightenment is not about love and light.* For those who choose not to look away from what they fear, it will be the greatest work of their lives.

"Understanding the Hyperdimensional Matrix Control System is key in this day and age for anyone who wants to awaken and have a better world. Sincere self-work and de-programming oneself from consensus reality is also part of it to essentially connect with our spiritual nature — your sovereign embodied true self, connected to the Divine in order to transcend the mutant Matrix and activate your original blueprint prior to the "fall" from your true state of being via genetic modification. This is the Great Work. It is not an easy path and work, for it entails facing our fears and questioning our deep-rooted socially / cultural conditioned beliefs and programs. Disillusionment is an inevitable part of the process, but the only way out is through."

-Bernhard Guenther

CHAPTER 7:
THE WHOLE INSIDE

"To land in the body as come to rest in the present is to return to the richness of being - which in some way is always enough."

- PHILIP SHEPHERD

As I continued walking towards my mountain, for the first time in my life I knew I was traveling with my greatest companion, despite being alone. This new acquaintance with mySelf filled me with inspiration and curiosity. With my spirits high and clutching my new gunny sack, I ventured through the last of the valley of the shadows and darkness. The canopy overhead became thinner and more sunlight shone through, kissing my skin. I felt the sun energizing me in a way I'd never noticed before. My skin was supple and soft to the touch; it felt new and fresh, as if I'd been reborn. The terrain became more vertical and the dampness of the jungle began to fade. The foliage was changing ever so slightly, and the trees began to give way to shrubs. With each step, I noticed how strong my legs felt, how each move I made seemed to be painless and without effort. I didn't have to think about my next foot placement because my body could feel where it needed to go. It felt great and I relaxed, allowing my body to take over while I remained present to all that was around me. The mindless marching and the deep connection to my body felt empowering. As I focused on just being in my body, I realized how exhausting constant mind chatter really was! I arrived at a clearing where I saw flattened grass. It looked as though a herd of large animals had bedded down the night before. As I sat on the grass, I could still feel the warmth of the herd that must have left just before my arrival.

I lay back for awhile, watching some wispy clouds making their unhurried way across the blue skies. Suddenly realizing my hunger, I grabbed for my gunny sack from the medicine women. I pulled out a large piece of ripe fruit and bit into the juicy flesh. As my upper two front teeth sank into the skin, juice slid down my neck and onto my chest. I didn't care to wipe it off; I was too focused on the pure bliss from this piece of nourishment. I had never eaten a piece of fruit this way before. I thought of the tree that had used the bounty of the forest around me to make this beautiful fruit, feeling my connection to that tree and gratefully receiving the goodness from the fruit. I cherished the fertility of that tree and the nourishment of the food. Then I noticed the seeds inside the fruit. I instantly realized how the bounty of the forest is a self-replenishing process if it's not interrupted or disrupted. Just one seed had the potential to produce hundreds more fruit like this one. When I was done, I went to the edge of the clearing and buried the seeds in the earth there. I blessed the seeds and gave gratitude for the nourishment I'd received from the fruit.

I set off again and soon came to a small stream. I followed the stream uphill, chasing the sound of a roaring river. Looking up, I saw many small streams appeared to converge further up the hill. As I neared, I could hear the sound of a great waterfall. Rounding a corner I finally saw it, and the power of the water took my breath away! The rocks were covered in green moss that was moist from the spray of the falls. Everything here felt more *alive* today. I could sense the undercurrent of the presence behind all of it. From the leaves of plants to the small animals skittering in the undergrowth, to the knots in the trees and moss that grew on the rocks of the river, I felt an aliveness in all of it. With a jolt, I realized the same power that animated these things also animated me, and that it's all connected, including me. It felt like the whole forest had eyes and could see me, just as I saw it, alive and beautiful. As a breeze blew in, I heard a whisper through the trees. It told me I had a home wherever I went, that I could always find safety and shelter if I sought it. I only have to take care of the plants and creatures that I come in contact with and they will take care of me. Sometimes "taking care" means respecting the distance and boundaries that some plants and animals require, just as I sometimes require distance too.

The cool waters called to me and I took off my clothes and began stepping carefully over the jagged rocks. Suddenly, the force of the water pulled me into its deep pools. It took my breath away. It was a shock to my system and I gasped for air, but I sensed that I was perfectly safe as long as I remained relaxed. I felt the energy I was receiving from these cold, replenishing waters. It washed over me and stripped me of any remaining traces of worry I'd been harboring. I sensed I was being washed clean in more ways than one. As I remained immersed in the water, I begin to tremble. Not from the chill of the waters, but from the washing away of old pains and regrets from my past. I sank into the core of my being and allowed the sadness and pain to leave my body. I could feel where I'd stored this pain and sadness within. Finally, letting it all go, I watched it wash down into the valley of shadows. I felt relieved. I had never been this singularly alone in the world and yet did not feel lonely here. Slowly I crawled out of the pool beneath the waterfall and made my way to a flat, sunny rock. I lay naked on this rock, letting it warm my bones and breathe heat into me. With my face to the sky, I could feel the sun kissing every part of me. It felt deeply soothing. I took a deep breath and tasted the moist air in my lungs. I was aware of oxygen flooding into my body and could feel my heart pumping this beautiful, clean air throughout my entire system. I sat up and breathed deeply until I lost track of the time. For the first time in my life, I had a sense of complete peace. I was wholly content with myself. Although I didn't know what was ahead of me, I no longer felt the dull ache of wanting anything. I felt complete.

●

The journey to awakening our wholeness is nothing short of miraculous. It's one of the most challenging and rewarding quests a person can take. Remembering the journey back into ourSelves is to relish and marvel at the brilliance of the being we are. After a lifetime of living out of alignment and in constant struggle with ourselves, we take a breath and gently whisper, I am listening. *I am listening to what you need.* One of the greatest gifts you can give yourself is to offer yourself unconditional love, fully and wholly.

Did you know you are the greatest love of your life? In this Truth, we discover most of what we have longed for in our loneliness is actually a connection to ourSelves. For some, this realization is uncomfortable and this part of the journey can be lonely. But within these feelings of loneliness, the Truth of your own connection to yourSelf is waiting to be remembered. There is a considerable amount of time needed in self-reflection to be in this part of the work. It's the practice of your life. A greater level of independence is achieved because you become your priority. I call this part of the practice "alone versus lonely." Some of our deepest patterns reveal themselves as we observe the need to reach out and find a connection with others to avoid being with what's within. This keeps us in a perpetual state of being without, of craving connection we don't feel, and keeps us in an endless loop of desire and avoidance. This was one of the biggest patterns I myself had to look at. For me there were times when being lonely made me feel as though I was drowning, and I would do *anything* to get someone to swim out and be with me. Anyone that did swim out to help me would quickly be pushed under the water by my incredible need and would either drown or leave me again.

The intensity of Truth, when you sit with loneliness, will shine the brightest light on our avoidance strategies. Often we search for connection as a distraction. Tinder, Plenty of Fish, and other dating apps and websites offer a "quick fix" to our lonely feelings, but the encounters found there often lack any depth, and then we are once again craving real connection and starving for genuine affection. Of course, not all connections made via these apps lack depth, some people even meet their partners this way, but the majority of the interactions are from a place of unconscious wounding and loneliness. Sexual addictive tendencies also stem from this need and resistance cycle.

There's a significant difference between being alone and being lonely. When we can embrace the quiet and connection that happens within ourselves, we then understand we do not need to be lonely, because we are always with ourSelves. We can be just as comfortable being alone as enjoying the company of others. When we are endlessly seeking connection from outside to avoid feelings on the inside, we end up on a life-long mission to try and fill the hole inside. But the only thing that can fill it is your own Wholeness. You can't escape the feeling and nothing outside of you will ever fill it. You can't keep running away, as it will become more and more painful to do so. Some people literally numb themselves to death, because they can't bear to feel the pain, as in the case of fatal alcoholism or drug addictive tendencies.

Wholeness comes from within. To connect, to breathe, and to feel yourself just as you are, offers the journey into embracing the relationship you have with yourSelf. When was the last time you kissed yourself? Have you ever kissed yourself? Try it now. Kiss the back of your hand. Feel your lips against your skin. What does it feel like? Do it again, and this time let your hand kiss your lips. When we live from this level of Self, we connect into what is true. We stop living just to get to the next thing. Instead, we learn to become present in each moment and embrace it. For me, learning to be comfortable in the Truth of my blues and all my hues of feeling required me to learn to sit quietly with myself, even when I was lonely. Denying our natural state of being is the ego telling us we need to be a certain way, but then we are missing out on all that is waiting in the present. Learning how to be with our emotions is one of the most organic processes of being human.

Jeff Murphy says, "You don't need to justify your feelings to anyone, not even yourself." In this space of not needing to justify, we can begin to connect back into our Self-worth. It becomes less about needing others to see us and more about what we need to see within ourSelves. When we can see ourSelves more deeply, noticing the divine within, we become more embodied in our true nature. Most of us spend a lifetime fighting against this nature when it would be much more beneficial to sink into it. However, within the very friction of the fight awaits our truest unlimited potential. It's never too late to begin.

When we are able to sit with our darkness, we also open the possibility to experience more light; *unbelievable light!* For me, to get to my light was quite a journey. The work that was needed to bring me here was incredibly deep, and at times challenging. However, I had no idea how amazing, blissful, and joyous life could be when I began embracing my Wholeness. The amount of light you can experience is in direct proportion to the amount of darkness you can sit with. This is what it means to become an expanded human and to feel all the hues of emotion. I am a person who struggles with incredible depression and anxiety, and I used to react to being in this state rather than simply being with it. When I was finally able to find a deeper level of Wholeness, I realized I didn't need to classify the days I'd experienced depression. I didn't need to assign labels to them, such as happy days, sad days, or any other kind of day. I could simply be present to the emotions I was experiencing in that moment, existing in my natural state. *Not needing it to be something different.* Instead, being present to what was true. Then I could hear the whispers of what the experiences were trying to tell me. I firmly believe that creatives, entrepreneurs, and trailblazers have an expanded capability for deeper feelings, which gives them access to creative superpowers. I don't see depression and anxiety as "bad," rather I see them as part of the spectrum of human emotions. My depression was a gift that showed me how to access the depth of my Soul, so I could create from a deeper place of being.

A profound realization I had came the day I simply stopped fighting my feelings. Innately my body wanted to lay in the fetal position, and for weeks I fought it. When I finally succumbed to giving my being what it needed, a great understanding came. I now see that I continue to grow into my higher Self on these deep and heavy days. It's my body's way of processing the download of information that comes as I move into my expanded Self. I finally understood that I could lay in the fetal position until my body no longer needed to lie that way. Within this surrender was immense expansion and healing. We needn't fight our body's own responses. For example, when we're "under the weather" our body is simply reacting to something within itself, or outside itself, which has affected it, and is responding accordingly. The body has an innate ability to heal itself. When we fight that natural response, we are focusing on the symptom instead of asking our body what it's responding *to*. If we focused on the root cause of our illness, we would understand the trigger for the disease and allow healing to take place. Whether it's a physical virus or a plague of the mind, we need to learn to treat the cause. Additionally, when we react to our emotional states, we are simply feeding into the cycle of disease.

To set out on the quest from a place of Wholeness requires us to sit in the alchemical process of what is True. Alchemy is more than just the changing of matter from one state to another. It is a living, breathing process of creation, a profound transformation, and magic. *Everything* in our world is experiencing alchemy all the time. If you look at any part of life you will see that everything is involved in a process of some kind. Just as with the trees, the animals, the oceans, and the grass that grows, our bodies are in a constant state of evolution, which occurs through alchemy. Being present to the whispers of the body allows us to become aware of the Mystery of life around us. When we understand the direction in which we believe we are meant to go and we accept the quest, it's important to remain present to the cues and directions from the Universe. They are always guiding us and course-correcting us to where we need to be.

Often we have tunnel vision regarding our goals and are not present to the subtle cues from Spirit. I understand the importance of having a vision and understanding the steps needed to achieve the vision. It's a starting point which offers us a course to follow. But if we stick to it rigidly, without allowing ourselves to be influenced and guided by Spirit, then oftentimes it takes us to a place where we aren't meant to be. We deny the body's responses to our chosen course (that would provide wisdom about whether we're headed in the best direction) because we are too busy coming from a place of ego and clutching to fill our human desires. We worry if we veer or change course at all, we might miss out. In this state, we are not embodied. When we do listen to the body's responses, we begin to embrace that perhaps what we thought was the path, and so vehemently clung to, wasn't actually meant for us at all! This can be hard to hear if you've gone all-in on a precious dream you perceived was for you. However, the wisdom of your body will not lead you astray; rather it will guide you to your highest path of expansion and evolution, away from the struggle when you're walking a path that isn't meant for you. This isn't an invitation to give up on your dreams, sit back on the sofa, and be completely apathetic; it's a prompt that can help channel your passion and energy in the best direction for you, finding more flow and enjoyment in the process. The Spirit guided path is the absolute highest choice.

We can then relish in the joy of missing out (JOMO). Missing out on things that aren't in alignment can cause distraction at best - burnout, suffering, and disease at worst. Learning to discern and when to say no is just as important as knowing when to say yes. There's power in how we choose to spend our energy. Our energy is one of our most precious resources and we must learn to say no to things that don't serve our Dharma.

When we set out on the path in Wholeness, attuned to our bodies, we are able to connect into the ability to be guided by our higher calling. This requires awareness, acceptance, and a willingness to embody the Truth integrating into our lives every day. In turn, this allows us to be present to ourselves without numbing our responses and allows us to direct ourSelves and our decisions using our internal compass. Our intuition and internal connection guide the way. The bonus is this is a much more enjoyable way to navigate life, albeit challenging at times. In each moment, we are presented with the opportunity to choose this new way or to fall back into old patterns. This is often connected to our desires of what we *think* we want and need when we're not present and listening. Embodiment requires us to act from our higher Self and observe what we're being guided to do. There's no greater act of self-love than doing what is best for ourselves, as opposed to what it is we think we want. Often our *wants* derive from that gaping hole inside that's waiting to find healing. With our wants, we are constantly trying to fill the void. Inside the void is a level of Truth that can support us on our path of stepping into Wholeness. Learning how to sit in this place and experience it just as it is, with all of its feels and moans and wanting, can shift the deepest patterns and bring levels of peace we have never known.

As we remember how to love ourselves, it's essential to have inspiration. Knowing how we find inspiration is a key that unlocks great power within us. For some it is found in books, others find it in nature, and some find it deep within while sitting in meditation, or simply being. People talk about mindfulness all the time, but what's missing is a deeper connection into our bodies. True embodiment and being present involves a connection with not only the mind but with both the heart and the pelvic bowl as well. Deep within our pelvic floor is a wellspring of connection and knowledge, a connection with the Divine. True embodiment comes from having a relationship with the pelvic bowl, heart, and mind. This trinity allows us to blaze our own trail in Wholeness.

To live in this expression of ourselves is a practice we must choose every day. Honest Self-expression and embodied Truth is the path for many, but it isn't easy living in this level of Self-awareness. It requires us to stay connected to what is happening around us, all the time, and develop an understanding that the process of us stepping into our Truth is fluid. Life is fluid. What we uncover about life and ourselves shifts our own Truth. Staying connected to all of it takes great skill, practice, and willingness. This skill can be mastered over a lifetime. *When we are present to life and we know ourselves, we are truly living.* Simplified living offers a freedom that comes when we want nothing.

"I love you, I am listening.
When is the last time you closed your eyes and said these words to yourself? When was the last time you took the time to give to yourself what you endeavor to give others? I love you, I am listening."
– Sarah Blondin

CHAPTER 8:
THE CHOICE TO BE NAKED

"Love is consciousness."

-S. PRIER

The sun went behind a cloud and I felt the change like a giant shadow looming over me. The sudden absence of the sun was a stark reminder of how precious the sunlight is, and how cold the earth would be without its warmth. Goosebumps appeared on my arms and legs, my naked skin chilly. I smiled, remembering when I was a kid and I thought my goosebumps looked like chicken skin. My skin was dry from the water and had turned a pinkish color from basking in the sun. The shadows and light danced across me as the clouds played hide and seek with the sun. A stiff breeze blew and I knew it was time to get dressed and continue on my way. I could now see that my skin was more of a red hue than pink, and it felt tight and uncomfortable as I moved around. I was sunburned, especially on the places that didn't usually see the sun. I stumbled around, agitated by the burn. I found my socks and shoes, but I couldn't find my clothes or the gunny sack with my food. I knew I'd left them next to the rock, but they were nowhere to found. "What the fuck? I know it was right here!" I said out loud. In the distance I heard a scurrying noise in the bushes. It was the sound of an animal. I ran after it only to find myself at the base of a steep cliff. Looking up I saw a small creature climbing the cliff face, struggling to carry something. It was hard to see what it was, but I was willing to bet it was my stuff!

I ran back over the rocks and put on my socks and shoes. I could still hear the animal fighting its way to the top of the cliffs. I leapt onto a rocky outcrop ready to climb up the cliff. My balance was shaky and my skin was pulsing with sore heat. A surge of pain ran up my arms and legs and I cringed from the burn. Not concentrating, I made a wrong step and my naked body fell across the jagged rocks. The pain seared my burned skin as I scraped my chest and belly. I was bloody, naked, and sunburned. Suddenly, a few feet to the right of me, a piece of fruit fell from the cliff above. As I looked up I could now see the animal clearly, up near the ridge. It was a small red fox, and it had torn open my gunny sack and was eating my food! I needed to get to the top of the cliff to get my clothes back, and whatever was left of my food supply.

Faced with my own limited human abilities and the tenderness of my naked flesh, I looked at the steep cliff face and wondered how that small creature had managed it. I had no choice but to face the fact that once again I had nothing. I felt like giving up, but then I remembered the lessons from my medicine ceremony in the forest and the advice from my spider and from Grandmother. I knew I must continue onward, facing my fears head-on. I took my first step onto the steep cliff and reached for the first handhold. I hoisted myself onto the first large ledge. This action somewhat reassured me of my capabilities. Despite my burnt skin and the scrapes on my tender stomach and chest, I continued up, navigating the cliff face and various ledges. I climbed higher and higher, but then made the mistake of glancing down. It sure looked like a long way to fall! The thought of failure loomed once again in my mind, and the fear and adrenaline were palpable in my body. Vertigo and dizziness washed over me. I panicked, clawing and grabbing at anything I could, all my muscles tensed. I'm going to fall! I held very still on the rock edge and slowed my breathing. Then, using the last of my strength, I managed to swing myself up onto a ledge where there was room for me to perch.

I looked out over the large dark valley I had traversed, and in the distance, I could see the original mountain I'd chosen to leave behind.

Thinking back over all the obstacles I'd already overcome, and the decisions I'd made to get me to this point, gave me the clarity to see myself in this present moment. I realized I was at an important junction in my journey once again. The truth dawned on me; I must raise the courage from within to continue. Giving up was not an option! I regained composure and pulled myself up yet again, this time finding myself on a larger ledge with a beautiful group of succulents that I hadn't been able to see from the river. For a moment I lost myself in the beauty and geometric perfection of the succulents. Each plant was unique and grew in its own way, but when I looked at the patch as a whole, they all fit together perfectly. As I relaxed a little, I realized I would stop at nothing to reach the top of this mountain; and with this, strength returned to me. Shaking, I stood up, determined to go on.

As I continued my ascent, each new handhold. I grabbed seemed to be smaller than the one before. My body began to ache, and as the sweat trickled, it stung the cuts and scrapes on my burnt skin. My hands were cut by the rocks, but I was so grateful to have my shoes! I was about two-thirds of the way up the cliff face when I heard a clamor from above. Small pebbles fell and as I looked up I could see the fox skipping across the rocks above me with my bag in its mouth. I watched as it leaped off a boulder the size of a large basketball. I saw the rock dislodge and begin to wobble. Lots of small rocks around it fell, hitting my head. In nightmarish slow motion, the large boulder began to roll down the cliff towards me. I was fully alert to the present moment and therefore was able to tuck myself in under a slightly over-hanging rock, just in time for the boulder to fly past my right shoulder. Thank goodness I had the presence to act quickly. Moments before, my head had been right in the path of the falling rock!

By now, the fox had made it up the cliff and was sitting contentedly at the top, once again feasting on my food. Angry at the fox for taking my supplies, endangering my life, and nearly killing me, I climbed over the last large outcrop with a new burst of energy. The adrenaline coursed through my veins and helped push me up the last bit of the cliff. As soon as I reached the grassy hillside, I picked up a rock and began searching for the fox that by now had disappeared again. I saw movement in the bushes nearby and saw my bag was caught on the underbrush. As I walked around the bush to retrieve my bag, I spotted the fox. I threw my rock as hard as I could toward the fox's head. Ever alert, the fox saw me coming and darted off, leaving my bag hanging in the bush. The stone missed the fox's head but caught it square in the rib cage. The fox let out a loud yelp, and I felt a bit guilty then.

I ran over to my bag to see what food was left. The fox had dug around in my clothes and only taken the food from the bag. As I scrabbled through the contents of my gunny sack, I found that some of the fruit had become wrapped up in my clothing and had been saved. I immediately felt a deep pang of remorse for hurting the fox. I realized all of us, humans and animals alike, are in this world trying to survive and that others can harm us without meaning to. It occurred to me how easily we impact each other's lives. While I put my clothes on, I thought about how hard I'd thrown the stone; it could have easily broken the fox's ribs! With deep shame, I realized I'd hurt a small creature because of my anger and fear about survival, and she'd just been going about her day! She wasn't trying to harm me. It became clear to me how easily we can hurt and be hurt by others, especially when we're acting unconsciously and out of fear!

●

We each have personal lenses through which we perceive the world, and we each choose how to experience it for ourselves. "Living Your Truth," is a term that's thrown around a fair bit in the personal development industry today. But the meaning behind it is so much more than the words. When we are committed to living this way, it's a completely different experience. It is one thing to feel the Truth of our existence and follow guidance while things are going well, but it's something else to remain present and trusting when things don't appear to be going smoothly. When we're dealing with the more unpleasant Truths and sitting on a pile of stinking, steaming emotions - when we have to tell someone we no longer love them or we treat them poorly because we don't understand or respect their choices - that's when it's harder to remain in Truth. Just because we don't agree with another's choices, doesn't mean we don't love them. It takes great discernment and many mistakes to learn to walk this fine and delicate line of Truth. Some people believe "speaking their truth" means they get to be a jerk - saying whatever they feel in the moment, regardless of how it affects others. But this isn't living in Truth, it's living in ego. There's an added piece that needs to be considered: Speaking your Truth *with Love.* When you speak your Truth with Love, you think about how what you communicate will affect the other person. The secret is learning how to share the Truth with kindness and compassion. "It is awkward before it is elegant." - Gina Devee

In my life, I've often been given the arduous task of telling people things that are hard to hear. It isn't something I would have signed up for, but I do understand it is part of my path. It's also one of the ways I choose to support others as a Coach. It requires a lot of consideration and discernment to be able to understand when it is my place to share my opinion or feedback because it was requested or needed within the coaching relationship, or when it's my own ego being triggered that makes me want to say something. We all have to do this work in communicating with the people around us every day. I always find that taking time before I act upon something offers the best solution. When we listen to the quiet of a situation and do not react immediately, we can find valuable information, although it's not always easy to do. While I was learning this new way of communicating, I often would wait twenty minutes before I would respond to something difficult someone had said. Experience offers wisdom, and now I wait a minimum of a day to reply! It's amazing how this space will offer proper insight to understand if my feedback is really necessary; often, the situation will resolve by itself.

Recently the world of social media has given everyone the ability to share and voice their opinions about everything, whether they were requested or not. It's fascinating how many times a day I observe people giving others unsolicited advice, and hurting them in the process. People often feel as though they have the authority to tell others how they should do things, and are quick to tell them what they believe "isn't right." We've lost the ability to support each other in seeing and expressing the Truth through our individual, unique lenses of life. When we dictate to others how we think they should express, speak, and behave, we lose our curiosity and our ability to find solutions and grow together. Often interactions require us to share information that, if not done considerately, will be completely rejected by the other person. No one can hear when they feel criticized. There's an art to sharing our Truth as we see it. We must be capable of feeling what arises and not be triggered to react to it. It can cause us to sweat and to feel nervous or nauseous. When we are in fear of triggering, or "flicking," the other person, we are not living freely and aren't comfortable being vulnerable.

The new age movement has people believing life is only about feeling happy; happy all the time, like we're a bunch of damn robots. Real, raw thinking and feeling are often labeled as negative. The new-age thinking portrays being "spiritual" as living in an elevated or high vibration state, where we are all entitled to absolute abundance - where every whim and desire is fulfilled if we just believe enough and if it doesn't it's because we didn't manage to hold the vibe or stay in the vortex. The problem with this is that's it's dysfunctional, disconnected from our Mother Earth and the guidance of Spirit, and it doesn't work! It's an attempt to paint over certain states of being that are deemed unacceptable, yet the reality is they are still present on earth today. That's the Truth of it and we can't cover it over with rainbows. Many followers of the new age movement often put so much energy into their efforts to raise their vibration and practice the law of attraction that they are broke, exhausted, and bitter. But there's no permission in this space to show that; they will be accused of not being in the right state, so their lack of results is their own fault because they were doing it wrong. I know this because I've been there. Nothing flowed for me until I completely dropped this insane struggle and went with the flow of life, trusting Spirit would guide me where I needed to be and taking actions as appropriate. Additionally, we don't control the time it takes us to step into power and ourSelves. It takes the time it takes.

During the California gold rush in 1848, the majority never found gold and the people who made serious money were the ones selling the tools to find the gold. Often the people who are making money in today's personal development industry are the ones showing others how to make money and teaching the law of attraction, but rarely do these approaches make their students rich. It works for some, but they are simply cookie-cutter replicas of their role models and they lack individuality. Often, they will find themselves unfulfilled in any success they have created because it didn't come from their Soul, it came from what they thought would sell.

The new age movement has normalized "manifesting" our desires. This is actually a disguised and cryptic way for the unconscious ego to perpetuate materialism and consumerism. We're constantly manifesting more, more, more, while completely disembodied from ourselves and with no notion of when we have enough. It's a disease masquerading as spirituality, which is celebrated and idolized, but it's one that is costing the resources of our Mother Earth dearly. Our need to constantly manifest more keeps us disconnected to what is real in the moment. A state of perpetual *doing* keeps us from experiencing just *being*. People are always resistant to this concept at first: how can we create our best lives if we aren't focused on our desires, manifesting, and doing? It brings up fear for many. What would happen if we just stopped? What would happen if we let go? We are afraid that our world will crumble, and often it does, but only to make way for a better world with less strife and striving. The secret is understanding we can still create when we are not in such a state of frenzied doing. We can still make magic that will be aligned with our Soul, rather than pushing from our unconscious ego. It comes from a deep place of Truth inside, instead of from the ego.

Being naked requires feeling deeply into each moment. It brings awareness of our true state of being right now. We don't always want to look at reality. Perhaps it's not as we wished it to be. The moment when we meet our true state, the reality of what is right now, we tend to run or create a story to deflect it. Sometimes we choose to go into victimhood, making excuses or lashing out in anger. Perhaps our inner dialogue about ourselves becomes harsh and judgmental. We assume the favorite role which we know how to play, whether it's victim or bully, and we think we are not enough. Often we are living in the illusion that when we can't manifest exactly what we want, it reflects negatively on us as people, highlighting some shortcomings of our personality. Like children, we take it personally, with no consideration that perhaps this is how it needs to be right now, and that it may even be in our best interest. Hindsight sometimes reveals this, and sometimes it will take more than a lifetime for Truth to be understood.

There's a disconnect between what we are capable of and how we think we get there. What most people don't understand is that in the naked Truth we see ourselves clearly. We see our lack of skill because we haven't taken the time to learn, we see our lack of understanding because we haven't practiced Self-inquiry, and we see our failings because we're no longer masking them by using the law of attraction (focusing on our desires and using affirmations as soon as we feel bad). All of these things keep us in a future-focused state, never present to the moment. There is a place for co-creation; the paradox from the true spiritual teachings is it happens naturally when we no longer care about the outcomes - when we've let go, surrendered, and become unattached. When we're guided by Spirit, then co-creation becomes a natural phenomenon, is in-flow, and can often be fun. It's in harmony with the world around and enhances our environment, instead of depleting it. This occurs when we're willing to meet reality exactly as it is right now, without all the roses and rainbows.

We live in an age of distraction. Most people don't follow through or finish things because they can't sit in the Truth of what it takes to achieve what they're going after. They will find a thousand ways to distract themselves from the task at hand and then make excuses for why things aren't working. This was probably one of the biggest parts of my own work. I had no idea how much I distracted myself when it came time to do something important. I would often spend hours getting ready to do something, but when it came time to take action, I didn't. I would need to eat something, make tea, or go to the bathroom. I would check Facebook, my emails, or whatever the preferred distraction of the moment was. I would do this until I ran out of time to do the thing I'd scheduled. Then I would complain that I never had enough time or money! It's funny looking back on it, but sadly that's how most people live today and then they wonder why they never experience the important things. I could never understand why I sat at my desk most of the day but never really accomplished anything. The pattern was deep in my life and in my lineage, and it took time sitting in plant medicine to finally learn how to go through the discomfort of creating things that were challenging for me. The only way out is through.

I was left with no more excuses, only my ability and my Self to rely on. The truth was, I didn't trust that I could do it. This lack of trust in myself led to spending more money on trainings, coaches, and programs. But, no matter what I learned, I felt I needed to learn more. The Truth is I didn't need to learn more, I needed to understand how to sit in my feelings and create something anyway. I needed to trust in myself and that I had something valuable to offer, just the way I was. Coaches, mentors, programs, and training can be fantastic resources to assist us on our journey; but when we come to rely on them instead of on our own internal guidance, it can be detrimental and even dangerous. The best training is the one which teaches us how to tap into the unlimited resources we all have inside. I was afraid of failing; but more than anything, I was afraid of succeeding. I was terrified of who I would have to become to start doing the things I said I wanted to do.

I hear so many people say they simply aren't inspired. Maybe that's true, but in my case, I didn't know how to work through it and create anyway. All the great creators of our time know that you start first, and get inspired second. In every moment we're attempting to create, we are succeeding, even when it looks like we're failing! Focusing only on the outcome is how we fail. Jumping into and relishing the process is how we succeed, regardless of the outcome. The thought of potentially failing often keeps people paralyzed, preventing them from ever making a start. Instead, they're looking around, hoping to find something out there that will bring them confidence and make them feel ready to begin. We are always seeking contentment, another course, or a guru to model ourselves after. The truth is, we never really feel ready. The trick is to start anyway! If we sat down with our naked Truth from the start and didn't get up until we'd made several attempts, we would figure it out. We'd create something, and then we'd course-correct. I experienced so much anxiety when I finally committed to writing this book. At times I was paralyzed by the worry of how it would turn out and what people would think of me. But, my brother said something profound to me. He reminded me it wasn't about how it was received - that's not my business. It's actually about me becoming the person who could write a book and share the Truth of my Soul, and who I would become in the process.

As I began the process of writing, I was aware of all of the things I was insecure about. Then one of the most powerful realizations of my life came to me: it wasn't about being done with the book, it wasn't about the end result. Waiting for me in every moment of this process was Truth and learning that would help me evolve, as well as new information and a deeper connection to myself. If other people also got something out of the book, that would be a bonus. I was present to the friction in my body and mind as I was writing, yet I was able to sit in it and write anyway, allowing that friction to ignite the fire of my creativity. One of my greatest powers is being able to work through the things that deeply challenge me, and still create despite these challenges. It's one of your powers too, if you choose to cultivate it. I now have such incredible gratitude for the practice I've developed through the work of sitting with my shadow as I created this book.

"I DON'T KNOW!" This is one of the most common replies I hear from my private coaching clients when I ask them challenging questions. We live in a society that causes people to fear being judged for saying the wrong thing, or for sharing commentary we haven't entirely thought through. We usually have a couple of seconds to formulate and offer a reply to a question. We're so disconnected from our bodies and feelings that it's easier to answer, "I don't know," than to say what comes up when we're unsure how our reply will be received. My reply to this is, "What if you did know?" (Techniques like these are called Natural Language Processing technique and it's only appropriate to use in accordance with natural law. The person you're talking to must be aware that you are using NLP in this situation.) Usually this elicits some annoyance, and often the annoyance grows to a deeper irritation as the cognitive dissonance grows. Regularly, the opinion of not knowing is argued for, but I believe our Souls always know. We simply need to be able to hear the answer from that deepest part of ourselves. It takes time to support someone into remembering how to know, how to feel, and how to understand what they really need. I am often surprised by how many people don't know what they want, despite living in a culture where people are stressed out, overwhelmed, in a constant state of striving for more, and it places a heavy emphasis on achievement. Yet many don't even know why they are doing it! People have lost the connection to what they need in the present moment, always thinking ahead towards achieving their goals. I believe if people sat in the Truth of the moment more often, we would have a healthier society with less need to over-consume.

Being emotionally and spiritually naked enables the ability to feel. It is the place where we find our deepest power, tap into our unlimited potential, and are unstoppable. We live from a place of trust and when we have moments where we feel doubt, we need to know how to sit with that and receive the lessons of that feeling. When we live like this, we're not in a place of needing to pretend anymore. Only then are we given the things we truly need in the present.

Facing ourselves in difficult situations is a true test of character. It acts as the gauge between who we think we are and how we act under duress. It's us, in our most naked and purest form. There's no denying it, as humans we are here as caretakers of the earth and all her beings. Life is about learning how to live in harmony. So how are we doing? Where do we need to improve? Figuring out how to live in this balance is part of the work of our lives. It's required to preserve life on earth. We don't know what we don't know, until we do. Then it becomes a choice of how we respond. Humans are finally beginning to wake up. What will your choices be now that you are awake?

CHAPTER 9:
THE REALEST LOVE

"Mystery and manifestations arise from the same source. This source is called darkness. Darkness within darkness. The gateway to all understanding."

-LAO TZU

As the sun began to set, a chill came over me. By now my clothes were a constant irritation to my burned skin. I knew I needed to find shelter for the night. I made my way into the thicker brush along the mountain's face, looking for a place to sleep. Soon I stumbled upon a fairy ring of small trees that had somehow endured the high winds. I crawled between two of the trees. Inside it was surprisingly quiet, the trees buffering the noise of the wind. It was a sanctuary, and the weather was no longer able to whip my tender skin. It felt peaceful, tranquil, and safe. The moss had grown so thick in places that I sank into a soft bed of green. Peeking through the moss was a small, familiar plant. It had many long stalks with small, gentle serrations along the edge. Deep in my mind, a memory stirred and my intuition told me I could use this plant for my sunburn. I hesitated momentarily thinking *what if it's poisonous*, but I had a strong intuitive hit that it was safe to use. I reached and broke off a large shoot of the beautiful plump, green plant. I opened the edge of the plant, where the serrations joined and began to peel off strips of the gooey flesh. As the moist strips touched my sunburned skin, I felt immediate relief. The cooling, soothing sensation gave me a flashback to the medicine women in the valley. This is the same relief I'd felt when I removed the bandages the women had put on my snake bite. Could it be the same plant?

Now that my skin was more comfortable, I pulled one of the last pieces of fruit from my bag and began to eat it, cherishing each juicy bite and the nutrition I received from it. I ate slowly and contentedly. As I was eating I became aware of the presence of something behind me, but when I turned around there was nothing there. Darkness crept over the treetops and I couldn't tell the source of the presence. It seemed as though whatever it was, it was circling outside the trees. I heard a twig snap and I whipped around. The fox was standing there, looking at me. She froze and didn't take her eyes off of me. Fear surged through me momentarily; would she attack me for hitting her with the rock? She didn't, she just stood there, gazing at me. Finally, after what felt like forever, her eyes slid over to the bag and then back to me. I noticed her ribs were sticking out and I realized how hungry this little fox was. Maybe it was because the fox didn't think of me as much of a threat, or maybe it was because she was so hungry; but despite clearly being afraid, she wasn't leaving. I reached into the bag to find some fruit for the fox. I grabbed a handful of berries and gently threw them on the ground in front of the fox. She sniffed them cautiously, and once she realized they were good, wolfed them down appreciatively and scurried away. I looked in my bag and saw a large mushroom I hadn't noticed before. I knew this mushroom was from the medicine women and wondered why I'd not seen it before. It was the last remaining bit of food I had. Despite my stomach rumbling, and not knowing where my next meal would come from, I decided to wait until the next day to eat the mushroom. I laid my head on a cushion of moss and exhausted, I drifted to sleep. It was a deep, delicious, and restful sleep. In my dreams the spider came to me once more, this time giving me the message to pay attention to the tricks. That was all she said and I didn't understand what it meant. *Pay attention to the tricks.* Who is going to play tricks on me? I wondered.

I woke up with the dawn. I stretched and let out a loud yawn. I had not felt this rested for ages. I rolled over to see the small fox curled in the moss on the other side of the clearing. She was resting, but had one eye open, carefully watching me. She still didn't fully trust me, and who could blame her? I thought about how hard it must be to survive out here, and how when food is scarce - it's every man and animal for himself! Foxes can be sneaky, I thought. Paranoia began to creep over me. Maybe it was the fox who was trying to trick me! *Would she try to steal the rest of my food?* In that moment it didn't occur to me that if she was going to do so, she would have done it while I was sleeping! My stomach growled loudly and I could only think of how hungry I was. In a state of fear, I grabbed the mushroom from my bag and greedily shoved it into my mouth. The fleshy texture felt good on my tongue and I had the sensation of being nourished and full from this one mushroom! I couldn't comprehend how such a small meal could make me feel so well fed. The fox got up and slowly came over to me, looking towards my bag, clearly hoping for some more food. She licked her lips expectantly and looked at me. Immediately I felt guilty, but I rationalized and told myself the fox had eaten most of my food; and anyway, she's a fox, she can easily hunt something!

As the sun began to warm the day, I leaned on a clump of moss and reveled in the comfort of this little sanctuary. I enjoyed the presence of the fox and the companionship she offered. I reflected on how the fox seemed so quick to forgive the past and my transgression in throwing a rock at her. She was simply present, living her life moment to moment, trusting her instincts. I noticed the strips of succulent still stuck to my sunburned skin and my thoughts shifted to the sensations in my body. Where the succulent touched my skin, I had the sensation of warming ice. I didn't feel the pain anymore, but there was a strong buzzing, tingling sensation from my toes to the tip of my skull. It was as if I could feel the energy field of my entire body, all at once. I could feel the fresh air filling my lungs, and it felt as though it was coursing through my veins as I took deeper and deeper breaths. Each exhale would send a pleasant tingle through my body, pulsing all the way to the edges of my being. I was so comfortable I didn't open my eyes for many minutes. I was lost in the sensations I was feeling.

When I opened my eyes, I could *feel* my surroundings too. Everything seemed crisp and clear, almost popping at me. I was aware of each wisp of the breeze and every hair on my arm that it touched. I could not only see the rays of sun between the leaves, but I could feel each beam of light radiating warmth. *It was as though I could feel the things I was seeing.* I felt a deep connection to everything I perceived. The trees felt like old friends around me and I felt secure and protected. I laid with my stomach exposed to the sky and my hands under my head. The clouds seemed to curl in on themselves and I could perceive the inner movements of each cloud individually. Like when you add creamer to coffee and the initial plume of cream bounces from the bottom of your cup and rises back up through the dark coffee creating a gentle swirling and twisting of the two contrasting liquids. I began to see some geometric shapes in the clouds and I enjoyed the sensation of watching them dance around each other. The beauty was almost too much to comprehend.

A few hours or so later, as my mind came back to earth, I realized I'd consumed a magic mushroom. The medicine women must have given this to me, knowing full well what it was. Then the realization hit me - I was out of food. I stood, feeling slightly wobbly. When I lifted my foot off the ground, I couldn't judge the depth of the vibrant green moss and I stumbled, lurching across the clearing to the tree line. My mind was playing tricks on me, and my spacial awareness was out of sync. Objects were further or closer to me than expected. I rested my hand on a small, sturdy tree and took some deep, refreshing breaths. As I breathed, I became aware of the strangest sensation. It was as though every time I exhaled, the tree that I was touching would inhale at the exact same moment, breathing in what I'd just exhaled. We were in sync. Then, all the trees began to breathe with me. My vision expanded, and I pictured my lungs as the earth's lungs. With each deep breath, I pictured the trees across the planet breathing with me. I was alive and connected. This had a stabilizing effect on me. Once I'd grounded myself by breathing with the trees, I realized I was famished. I looked around for my bag, but I knew I'd already eaten everything. Then I looked for the fox. She'd disappeared; I had no sense of time or how long she'd been gone. The sun was still high in the sky, but I felt lonely without my new companion and decided to look for her.

I left the ring of trees and the comfortable moss to search for the fox. Everywhere I looked, I thought I saw the fox scurrying away. I imagined I heard her footsteps in the wind but was unable to find where the sound was coming from. I continued climbing, higher and higher up the mountain in the hopes of spotting the fox. I noticed the air was becoming thinner. As the climb became steeper, I developed vertigo and stumbled over my own feet. I sat down carefully, fearful of falling back down the hillside. My mind spun off and I pictured myself falling down the hill. With this mental image came fear and anxiety. With a jolt, I brought myself back to the present with my feet planted firmly on the ground. I breathed deeply. I wasn't falling, I was alive and well. *I was alright.* Despite my fear of falling, I got up and continued on. I focused entirely on the path ahead and where to place my next step. I was so engrossed in my task, I almost forgot I was looking for the fox.

I noticed I was now about two hundred yards above the ring of trees, which I could now see was in a perfect circle. Just over the ridge, I found scuff marks in the soil. *My fox!* I followed the trail to a group of large boulders clustered together creating shade below. Walking into their shadow, I could feel the temperature change. With half my body in the shadows and the other half in sunlight, I marveled at the difference in temperature. The cold was claiming the left side of my body, as the right side was warmed by the sun. Inside my heart, I could feel a warmth I'd never felt before, yet I could also feel the cold coursing through my veins, bringing feelings of loss, grief, and death. The intensity of both feelings at once made me feel as though I was being blown open from the inside. It was more than I'd ever felt before, and I felt as though my body may shatter into rays of light. It was the most incredible love and the most intense loss I'd ever felt.

Visions of past lovers floated across my mind causing me to wonder if I'd ever known how to love. Then I remembered being very small and my mom chasing me around the house. I shrieked with laughter, and when she caught me she'd shower me with endless kisses. That felt like pure love to me.

Although this was different, I could still feel the stirrings of love when I thought of the fox. In this moment, I understood that the loss of love is how we understand what real love is, and the duality is necessary here on earth.

I wondered if it's like this in other realms. I felt like I was being kissed all over by a hundred loving lips, it was like petals brushing my skin. I realized I was being kissed by Spirit. This moment forever changed me and the way I understand love. I felt within me the capacity to love every being. Love is consciousness.

I stood in the sensation a moment longer until out of the corner of my eye I glimpsed a shape moving between the large rocks. As I looked closer, I saw it was the fox. Seeing her again filled me with a joy I can't explain. It was like meeting an old and much-loved friend after a very long time. Remembering our first meeting and how I felt when I hit her with the stone, I knew in my heart I'd never hurt her again.

Then I noticed the fox was eating something! Upon seeing me, the fox trotted joyfully over to me. She nudged my hand with her nose and circled me several times; clearly, she was pleased to see me too. She walked ahead, paused, looked back at me, took a couple of tentative steps, and looked back at me again, as though she wanted me to follow her. I begin walking and she led me to an area of loose earth underneath one of the rocks. Suddenly she disappeared into a small gap, just big enough for her to squeeze through. On closer inspection, I realized there must be a hidden cavern underneath the rocks. The fox soon came out with a large mouthful of food which she shyly dropped at my feet. I wondered how much food the little fox had stashed underneath this rock. Perhaps she wasn't starving after all! I picked up some berries she'd dropped at my feet and popped them into my mouth. They were perfectly ripe and sweet. I thought of the morning and the dream where Grandmother had warned me to watch out for tricks! I thought she'd meant the fox, but the reality was all along I'd been tricking myself by believing the fox had some malicious intent. The fox was just a creature, living by her instincts. She had no reason to intentionally harm me, *and* she had shown me great kindness! The fox only wanted to live her life and be exactly what she was; a red fox! The fact that she'd also shown me love made her a special fox in my eyes. I now realized all the events leading up to this point were somehow linked. It felt like a divine connection between me, the medicine, and my new-found friend.

●

Being in alignment with our Soul, and listening to Spirit, puts us in a position to trust in perfect timing. Patience and faith are required. This practice helps us understand what is meant for us, as opposed to living in the space of purely personal wants and desires. Most of our mental discord comes from not having the things we desire; but when we trust in the Divine, we know what is meant for us will come.

Living in Truth is living beyond the realms and rules of the boxed life. It is daring to stand out and not try to fit in. When we make these choices, we are left standing completely exposed for all to see. Even more importantly, as we stand there we feel this level of exposure, like emotional frostbite from head to toe. It's the courage that arises from deep within us when we choose to speak up when we push the words out even when it's hard and we're afraid when the voice is cracking and shaky. It's sitting alone in the depths of our uncertainty after we have said what no one wanted to hear. We must know ourselves on the most intimate of levels in order to forge the path ahead, the path that is meant only for us. When we know the Truth that is in our Soul, we are aligned with why we are here.

Walking this path requires incredible patience, as each step provides us a deeper connection to our stoicism and faith in our tenacity. The deeper we can sit with our Truths, discomforts, and realness without the need to complain or numb, the further we expand. This level of humanism requires that we have the ability to see ourselves clearly. We innately understand how to offer support and how to soothe others, and in walking this path we learn how to do the same for ourselves. Achieving this kind of Self-love takes great endurance. It requires us to go against what we've been taught and to find the answers within.

Achieving this level of responsibility and Self-love was one of the most frustrating lessons of my journey. I spent years trying to re-wrap this need into many different things. When what I truly seeking failed to show up, I attempted to convince myself and others I would settle for less than I really needed. The irony is that once I let go and returned to myself, everything I'd been chasing after came more easily - *only* once I was no longer attached to it! The resistance to the Truth only made it more difficult to let go, until finally, I had to remove myself entirely from the relationships that I yearned for most. Then, and only then, I was able to understand what I needed could only be found within.

I'm not suggesting we can't have relationships, go after our (Soul-guided) dreams, earn good money, and offer love and support to one another; but for me, there was no way I could have a deep connection with another until I was able to fully hold myself and fulfill my own needs. In this place of deep honesty, I was able to understand my level of need and how to bring soothing and healing to it. There is no greater way to know we are alive than to feel all that we are capable of feeling. We need to feel all the hues of emotion. Don't make it wrong; just allow it to be what is. From there, life will flow.

There comes a point when our need to give meaning to everything that happens is really just bypassing the truth. *Sometimes things just happen!* The stories we often create to understand events can serve a purpose in bringing awareness to certain patterns and issues in our lives, which may need attention. When we are simply able to experience life as an observer, rather than reacting to everything, we have begun our expansion. There's a trap to watch for here; we don't want to abdicate responsibility for our choices. Being an observer does not mean sitting passively on the side, or not taking responsibility for our actions. It simply means being present, observing ourselves and our situations, and taking a moment or more before responding. This practice is not about perfection. We are human, after all. There are times when we will still react unconsciously. The point is to learn from our reaction and notice what effect it created. Was it one we would choose again? As we progress, we may find we react unconsciously less often. We're able to take the moments as they come, not needing to label them and make something "wrong," "bad," "good," or "right," - instead, allowing a moment to be just as it is.

Incredible awareness happens when we simply experience something and let it pass through us without judging it. We have lived for so long with the idea that it's not acceptable to feel heavy or darker things. I spent a lifetime doing everything I could to avoid the depths of darkness waiting inside of me. Because of this avoidance, the heavy feelings pulled at me my entire life, draining me and making me sullen. The more I tried to bypass them, the more they pulled at my Soul; until they finally took me down. *It was needed.* I had spent a lifetime trying to avoid the very thing that would help me to finally feel ALIVE.

To be alive is the very thing we all yearn for. It's that itch that can only be scratched when we go inside ourselves. It is also the thing we fear the most; but to be alive, we must fully embrace all our hues. It always stuns me, the lengths humans will go to remain busy and avoid this process. *It's insane.* For most of us, we do our best to avoid conflict and keep the peace with others, all the while creating a war within. For some, they act out their pain in the world. Then, we label them as "bad" and "trouble-makers" and all kinds of other unpleasant labels. Perhaps in some ways, they are merely more honest than we are, choosing to express the pain and dysfunction on the outside rather than keeping it hidden. We continually feed ourselves information and use distraction to avoid the pain, ultimately trying to find any external thing to make us feel differently. We have become so gluttonous in trying to understand what it is we hunger for, we drive ourselves mad and over-consume. This continues to the point where we've had enough of the suffering. Then we look for another way, and eventually, we are left with no choice other than to dive into the abyss of ourSelves and face the darkness inside. This is a brave choice, and we don't know whether we will die, or grow wings and fly. In this moment, we are alive, not knowing what is next. We begin to trust that we will figure it out, and we will be guided. We trust we will be okay. In the darkness is where we encounter the awakening of our own power. In letting go of how we need things to be, we're able to connect into what is *meant* to be. There we discover peace and stumble across our own potential.

When we learn to trust ourselves completely, life opens up in a different way. Our inner world is understood and expressed as Truth out there in the world. We stop trying to push and make things different. When we can sit with what is true now, we find ourselves with less desire. What we are experiencing is perfect in all of its flavors and hues of emotion. To feel complete, fulfilled, peaceful, and Whole, we must first accept ourselves. We must be able to say, "This is me, now. The real me. I'm fine as I am. I see me and I love me. I am alive and I trust I will figure it out and that I will be guided by my Soul. I am home, and from this place I am Whole."

The essence of being alive is finding peace in all of it, in everything that happens. The secret is living in all the hues of life and surfing the waves that are brought to us. Love is one of the greatest expressions of life. When we are alive we feel the rapture that overcomes our being, yet in the next breath, we can feel the grim reality that one day this too will slip from our fingertips, as all things do. Nothing is supposed to be permanent because all of life is a process. Every bit. Things, people, situations, and money are not supposed to be grabbed or owned. It takes great trust allowing the process to unfold as we slowly learn to grow into a loving being. This process happens with everything - our spirituality, our ability to discern, our own understanding of ourselves, and how we treat others. All of these things take time to grow into. We find ourselves locked in the struggle when we think things can be held onto indefinitely. We have been taught we're *entitled* to live and to love, and so we treat them as things we're owed, rather than something amazing we may get to experience. We've lost our ability to marvel, to be in awe of, and to appreciate. Of course, we *can* experience love any time we choose to go inside. We may also decide to appreciate life for the gift that it is.

We are in a relationship with everything around us: how we choose to drink our water and how we eat is a relationship. We have a relationship with our clothes, our home, our neighbors, the way we brush our hair. In my life, I've spent a lot of time guzzling water down just to get in it. With maturity came the realization that how I choose to drink the water is equally as important as the drinking of it. It is no different than how I wipe my nose, put lotion on my skin, how I take a shower, and even how I wipe my bum! How we touch ourselves and take care of ourselves is a good indicator of the relationship we have with ourSelves. We often treat our own bodies in such a detached way. We would never treat a friend or an animal the way we often treat ourselves. This is especially true for how we treat ourselves and others when we feel sick, angry, or depressed. How we talk to ourSelves and treat ourSelves during these times is a big indicator of where we are in our work and practice of being an expanded human.

The word love has many meanings. The love we have for a furry friend, a family member, or an intimate partner, even the love for a special place which touches our soul. It can be a feeling we have, an action, or even a state of being! In many ways, the word love has become commercialized. It's overused for commonplace things, such as "I love chocolate" or "I love handbags;" so much so, the essence of the word is often lost. Some define love as intense feelings of affection. I think these attempts to describe the indescribable may give us a hint of what love really is. I'm not sure there are adequate words to truly express the potency of this thing we call love. Sometimes we feel we are "in love" with another. A breath taken in this state can be mesmerizing, jubilant, and exciting, and can take us to dizzying heights. However, when the other person says or does something we don't like, we can crash and feel pain, grief, and despair.

Others view love as intense feelings of passion, lust, longing, and even obsession; but these are not love, these are something else. Unrequited love is when we love someone, but that love is not reciprocated. It's another trick of the ego to avoid being with ourSelves and facing what's inside. It's focusing externally rather than internally and projecting our painful feelings onto another. Today, romantic relationships and marriages are more about egos trading, rather than an expression of real love. Relationships are a deal that's made - I mean, let's call a spade a spade. Sometimes true love can be present inside the deal, but if we are honest about what is really going on, we would admit that part of finding the Truth is being able to see what is really happening. And being able to express that Truth. From a place of Truth, real love is born. True love doesn't *need* anything. I believe true love is a state of being. It demands nothing; rather, it radiates out and warms those who come in contact with it, much like the sun warms the earth.

When we embrace a deeper level of Self, we understand what it means to exist in an embodied way. We understand the depths of our Souls and we begin to know how to love ourSelves. Then, we are truly alive. Only from this place are we able to grasp the magnitude of love. Human life is about feeling all the hues of emotion. The excited inhale when in the arms of our lover or the pain that comes with the last labored breath of a loved one passing.

Let's face it, the way we have been taught to love is pretty dysfunctional. It isn't *always* dysfunctional, but we've been taught that love is found in and from others, instead of from within ourSelves. There's no greater human experience than the tender love of a mother for her baby, the strong shoulder of a father or a brother when we're in need, or the tenderness in a kiss from a lover. But most of us are seeking a love that can only be found inside. The resistance to this idea is intense. It goes against our entire societal programming. I know I certainly wanted to reject this idea! How could it be that the love I was seeking was my own? Have you ever heard someone say, "I just want someone to love me the way I love?" This statement is interesting because people do not love the same way. The Truth underneath this statement is we are actually looking for the love that only we can give. We all desperately desire love from ourselves! When I want someone to love me the way I love, *in only the way I can give it,* I need to look no further than myself. Another cannot love me that way, because they are not me.

Our world is expanding. Love is evolving, and so is our capacity to understand the different kinds of love. Society is slowly becoming more accepting, allowing people to be honest, to express and live their Truth. I think we are just beginning to peel back the layers of the fruit to see the potential that Love is capable of. This process has to start with where we are and has to take into account the fact that there's still a lot of dysfunction that comes with our versions of love. Divorce is far more than just a statistic, it is the poster child that demonstrates the lack of consciousness we have about what love is and what it means to accept another. On the one hand, divorce means people no longer feel trapped in unhealthy situations, but on the other, it has made us quick to throw in the towel when we uncover our partner's flaws. When two people are brought together in a conscious relationship, it's the perfect environment for each individual to do their deepest inner work, the work that can only be done when we're with an intimate partner. But this isn't how the world currently sees relationships. We believe relationships are supposed to be perfect and happy all the time, rather than be what we need for our Souls to evolve. Our wounding and our need to project onto others often play out in romantic love. We have been disconnected from the relationship with ourselves for so long, we haven't learned how to love ourselves. How can we expect to find love with someone else if we don't know how to love ourselves? As we said, we are the greatest love of our lives. It sometimes makes me feel sad to realize I ignored this love within myself for most of my life, endlessly and recklessly trying to find it with another or within the confines of a romantic relationship. My true love was me the entire time! But I was in so much need, I missed it.

One of the shifts I've observed in my life is the idea that love is purely based on trust. That to love someone, we have to trust them. It's almost as though we buy into this boxed idea that if we agree to love each other within certain confines, then the trust will keep the relationship together. We say we will trust our partner if they do specific things and act in certain ways, but this leaves no room for the Truth of what is being felt or space to share difficult things with one another. This is why cheating and lies are so prevalent. Two people may agree to trust each other within a relationship, yet completely lack the ability to share their Truth with each other. Most (myself included at one point) don't even know what their Truth is. That's why we must do the work. It doesn't necessarily mean you have to leave your current relationship while you do the work, but it might. Only you will know.

In relationships and marriages, often people simply agree to what is expected, knowing they won't be in Truth. They do whatever is necessary to keep the appearance of a happy marriage while fulfilling their real desires in secret and breaking the promise to be in trust. This is because they don't feel safe to speak their Truth within the relationship. The missing ingredient in this recipe for love is we must be willing to show up in Truth. Not just once in a while, but in each moment of every day. To be able to share our experience of truth in partnership, and to share it with kindness and compassion, takes a considerable amount of personal work. It also requires being the person who can receive the Truth of what our lover or partner is sharing. Love and speaking the Truth is a practice. This level of communication offers access to a deeper experience of love and consciousness. It requires the ability to observe and not be in reaction. Conscious love is a living ceremony. Choosing to show up in Truth requires incredible presence and the ability to live in a fluid motion. Life isn't static. Living and loving is a flowing energy.

I believe shifting love into a space that is based on Truth is the recipe for conscious love. Our human experiences change and shift all the time. When we hold the expectation that a person or relationship needs to stay the same, the chaos begins. When we love ourselves, and our partners love themselves, we then know how to hold space for (and love) the other. Then we can be together in love. Wholeness must be found on an individual basis before two people can share in love this way. The journey one goes through to find this within is the greatest love story of our time. My hope is the new story that starts being told will set a new precedent in love.

When was the last time, during sex, you and your lover took a breath at the same time? When was the last time you felt truly connected while making love? Have you ever held eye contact the entire time you were being intimate with another? Do you understand the potential two people can experience together when both are coming from a place of Wholeness? Some might call it a true Soul to Soul connection. There's a chemical process that happens which allows incredible depths of consciousness which can only be shared at this level of connection. A burning away of shyness and inhibition, you might say. There's so much new-age crap that promotes sexual fantasy, sexual healing, or tantric teachings when realistically it is only feeding the unconscious ego. But there are ancient teachings that *can* help lovers traverse the intimate trails within. Discernment is key in knowing what to pay attention to. Your gut will know. If it feels sleazy, it probably is. You'll know true intimacy when you experience it; and although it won't always feel comfortable, your Soul will recognize it. Intimacy is a unique experience. Two conscious lovers have the ability to connect into magic only they can create. Sex, sexual intimacy, and love-making don't become routine for those with a conscious connection. The more creative we are using our own unique talents and gifts, the more we are able to connect into the unique alchemy of the union. One of the most incredible experiences I had was when a lover used the frequency of his voice to stimulate my body. This is an experience that could never be replicated. *It was its own magic.*

So how do we show up in Truth for our relationships? This is one of the most popular areas of work I cover with my private coaching clients. The idea that you can have what you desire within a relationship seems mind-boggling. All it takes is being the person who can show up in Truth. It sounds simple, but it's not easy. I often see people show up on dates and at the beginning of a new relationship who are out of alignment with their own Truth. They show what they think the other wants to see, rather than who they really are. They pretend to like things they don't in order to impress the other person. This seems harmless enough, but it leads to loneliness because the other person doesn't really know *you*. Often people desire to have more than one sexual partner or to date more than one person, but this isn't what they express for fear of being judged. They keep this part of themselves a secret, giving a false idea of who they are and what they want. This kills intimacy. It kills love. If we show up in our honesty from the beginning, we would avoid a ton of heartache.

Unfortunately, there's big business in this type of dysfunctional love. Women are primarily targeted and manipulated into buying programs and products that claim they offer the exact words to make a man love them, or that they can make your appearance a certain way in order to attract a man. Or they use "tricks" to make him fall for you. For example: "Make him fall for you, he'll never look at another woman again." "Get him back." "101 Tricks to Magnetize Him." It's manipulative and revolting. The worst part is this has somehow become the norm. It's more common to be left in the dark about what happened with someone we were dating, instead of both parties having said what they thought and felt. The problem is when we're busy using these techniques, we're not being present with the other person. There's no space for real intimacy to take hold and grow.

This is where the plague of online dating and hook-up sites factor in. Yes, I know, some people *have* met their partner on a dating site. I have friends who met their partner on an online dating site. It does happen. To those who have, all I say is, "Awesome." But, the truth of the matter is most people on these sites perpetuate unhealthy patterns based on some of our deepest wounds. I definitely fell into this trap. I thought I could force my way into love because I somehow deserved it. I had many disastrous dates because of this belief. Because I was so needy, I considered the idea of an open relationship, even though this wasn't my Truth. It's fascinating to see how far we are willing to manipulate ourselves into ideas that are not aligned with what we want, while at the same time trying to help ease the beast of loneliness. I personally do not participate in open relationships; however, I'm not against them. I think it's a choice each person and couple must make for themselves. It is something that requires an incredible level of honesty and truth.

The topic of open relationships comes up a lot in the work I do, especially with men. I believe an incredible level of self-work must be done before a person is ready to make this choice and fully understand the level of responsibility that comes with this decision. It's hard enough to love and be in Truth with one person, let alone many at once. It takes an evolved being to do it well. I do not believe the way open relationships are being portrayed as "the answer" in today's society is coming from a conscious or evolved place. I also think it's important not to judge someone who makes the decision to be in an open relationship. Having discernment about whether it's right for you is one thing, and understanding that bringing the Truth forward in a relationship is another. Personally, I would prefer someone to show up in their Truth, whatever it is, rather than not be open about their preferences and lie in an attempt to shelter the other person or avoid judgment. I am an advocate of Truth. My work is supporting people in being able to show up in, and share their own Truth with the world. *It has nothing to do with my own feelings about it.* So, what is your Truth in the area of love and relationship?

Stepping into this level of Truth and sharing certainly isn't something that happens overnight. It takes time for people to accept the Truth within, find their voice, and share it with the world. I think the most important part, as humanity begins to shift into this way of being, is to support one another in our unique understanding of Truth. To know this honesty requires a person to experience intense levels of emotions and to support each other in that. Conscious communication is the key that will help us learn to listen to each other without judgment. When a person opens up to this level, our experience or opinion often isn't what is needed. A person opens up much more when they experience being heard, without being criticized, judged, or compared to someone else. *This is holding space for truth.*

I dove this deep into love in this chapter because love is an integral piece of life. Love is life, and life is expanding. The way we understand love needs to expand with us. Consciousness itself is expanding. No one knows where any of this is headed. The only thing we ever have control over is our response. We can choose to hold space for the evolution of love, or we can remain in the space of expectation and attachment. We are here, we are alive. *Change is inevitable. Expansion is a choice.*

CHAPTER 10:
THE EXPANDED HUEMAN

"Grandfather, Grandmother Creator; makers of all things.
Let the people that need to find us, find us."
-BRIAN "BB" MELENDEZ

The sun was setting, and I decided to bring the food the fox had given me back to the ring of trees. I wanted to rest for one more night before continuing up the mountain. On my way to the ring of trees, the fox followed me, and I felt a sense of growing trust between us. The Truth was understood and we both knew we would be fed and watered. There is plenty for both of us. As I settled in my cozy resting place, I felt an overwhelming sense of comfort. I lay in the moss and stared at the sky overhead. Suddenly, I spotted movement. The clouds parted and a huge golden eagle emerged. It was far away, but I could tell this was a powerful bird. It dwarfed the other birds, flying higher than any of them. As it flew closer to me, I felt it was being drawn to me, and I was drawn to it. Soon, the eagle was circling above the ring of trees. I could hear his massive wings beating the air. He dove towards me and for a moment I met his gaze. An intense jolt went through my body, like a bolt of electricity sending me into another vision.

I envisioned a place where every fruit eaten was replaced by a tree that would bear more fruit. I saw myself with my hands in the dirt and my back to the sun. I could smell the fertility of the soil and feel the moisture beneath it. I saw myself planting many seeds, some to eat and others to make medicine. I felt at peace. I saw people and animals coming to join me in this new place. The fox was there, and she was content and well fed. This was a place of great Truth. A place where there is no fear of not having enough, a place with a sense of security and comfort in natural abundance.

The vision faded and I found myself in the clearing with the fox who was watching me, her fur blowing in the breeze. During the evening, the winds died down and we slept peacefully beneath a star-filled sky.

Upon waking, the fox and I left the moss-covered sanctuary. I knew I must press on. I kept thinking about the vision I'd had the night before, trying to rationalize it and tell myself it was all a dream, but I knew deep down it wasn't. This was a real place I must find. Through this quest, I learned to trust my own intuition and to not doubt the process. We exited the thick brush onto open hillside and the fox darted to the ridgeline, then turned and waited for me to follow. I followed his path and this time it was much easier than when I'd climbed the same hill the day before. We reached the large rocks and continued past them. The fox seemed to know the way, and we progressed for several hours in companionable silence. She would often sniff to find a game trail, where the grass was trodden by many different creatures. We stopped to eat at intervals, always planting the seeds from any fruit we consumed.

I could feel that we were nearing the top of the mountain because the valley looked small now. It was hard to believe I'd faced some of my darkest demons there. From this perspective, it looked like a green canopy and not like a valley of shadows! I looked for the golden eagle, but it was nowhere to be found. Without a cloud in the sky, I could see the original mountain where this journey first began. I thought, that which is behind me no longer serves me; I must stay present and move forward, but always keep the experience and wisdom from the past in my heart to guide me forward.

We continued on; the air became thin and I felt queasy. The vegetation was thinning, as was the wildlife. It seemed as though nothing wished to be this high. I knew in my heart I must get to the top of this mountain. The higher I climbed, the more difficult maneuvering became. The fox had to wait longer for me to catch up and my breath became shaky. I began to doubt myself again. Feeling weak, I almost collapsed. Resting my hand on a rock, I steadied myself. The fox nudged me encouragingly with her nose. She was urging me forward so I took another step, unsure if it would be my last. With her help, I navigated the last rocky stretch to the top. Awareness finally hit me that the fox is my truest Self. She had been with me, watching me, waiting for me to see her and to nourish her. I was chasing her, thinking she was tricking me; but I see now that she is the deepest part of me I needed to find. And now, I will walk with her on every journey to come. She is the greatest love of my life.

Finally, breathlessly arriving at the highest point, I felt a wave of pure exhilaration sweep over me. With a surge of energy, I jumped up and screamed, "YESSSS!!!!" while punching the air. My yes bounced throughout the valleys below and echoed back to me. My fox leaped excitedly, sharing in the glory. I looked around realizing for the first time I had a 360 degree view. It struck me that there were many, many mountains, all different shapes and sizes. The mountain range stretched as far as the eye could see, with peaks and valleys, wooded areas, lush meadows, rocks, streams, rivers, and cliffs.

I took a moment to let it all sink in, the fact that I was now somewhere I'd once hoped to be. I'd hit a goal, achieved something big. I went on a journey that has forever changed me. The lens through which I now viewed my life was different. As I appreciated this moment, basking in my own accomplishment, the colors around me were vivid and the patterns of Mother Nature's canvas framed my view. Reviewing my journey to this point, I realized everyone's journey is different and unique. Life is about finding our own unique mountain to co-exist with. No two paths to the top of the mountain are the same! No one will ever have the exact same experiences I did. No one will face the same challenges, feel the way I did, or see things the way I saw them. The struggle, the pain, the relief, the confusion, and finally arriving at a long-held goal; none of that can be experienced exactly the same way by different people.

If I had stayed on the original mountain, I may have made it to the top, but I wouldn't be living in my own Truth - nor would I have cultivated a deep, and loving relationship with my Self. I'd felt the call to climb my own mountain and it pushed me to understand parts of myself which I'd ignored my entire life. It showed me things about myself I'd never known before and helped me to discover my courage. It helped me to trust my own intuition, sit with my own feelings, face my darkness, embrace my awkwardness, and give myself the love I'd always craved. This journey has expanded me in ways I could not even begin to describe. Forging my own path and following my own Truth brought me to this point. It got me to the top of my mountain. But now what?

As I looked at the mountain peaks, I could see immense forests extending as far as the eye could see. On the right side of my mountain was a small valley about the same elevation as the ring of trees. I could see trees, plants, and lush grasses growing there. There was a gushing stream, and I could imagine the noises of animals foraging for food. *Home.* I knew that was the place from my vision earlier. That was where I would build a home for myself and continue to live in my Truth. I sat down and felt a smile spreading throughout my being. The fox curled next to my leg. I closed my eyes and let the sun's beams wash over me. As we sat, one final vision came to me: I'm in the same lush valley as before, my home, but this time other people are with me. We are all learning from each other, growing together, and sharing food. We exist in harmony with our surroundings and the animals among us. People come and people go; what I realize is each person in this place had their own mountain to climb, their own version of the journey I've just taken. Some people climb the same mountain, taking different paths; but all are learning. I wonder if the people who climb the same mountain are Soul families. Many people come to the valley I live in. They come to prepare for their own journey, to learn, to sit with me and the others, and to sit with their own emotions and discover their own Truths. They feel all the hues of themselves. They come to share in the strength of community. They come to give and take gifts, to swap tools and to be in partnership. Some come for refuge, midway through a quest. All who visit gain expansion.

All who come to the valley receive the valuable lesson that they can forge their own path; everything they need is inside them, and they will create their best way forward. Each individual experiences coming home to themselves. Many had to step through their own doorways of fear in order to reach their truth; but when they do, what they find on the other side is their pure potential. All leave with a renewed sense of possibility, an internal compass to guide them, and confidence in their abilities. They go into the world and express what they've learned, living and sharing the Truth.

In my vision, I saw a flash of energy expanding out from the valley, a purple light rippling across the world. The light of the Truth begins to illuminate all the dark corners of the earth. I see glimmers of hope for healing as humans begin to wake. Our Mother Earth can heal. We can heal. I see animals prick their ears, listening. They are ready. Finally, I know this journey has been worth it. Deep within my bones, I know I have found my way back home; to me, to Wholeness. This journey has led me to the place where I belong. The place meant for me. My vision ends; I turn my face to the sky and begin to pray before descending the mountain to my new home. My prayer is that everyone finds their way back to their home within to Wholeness. The call to climb the first mountain is the beginning of a long line of trials and tests that we all must face. How long we choose to experience that first test is up to each individual. We can only hear teh truth when we are ready to hear it.

●

Waiting for us deep within is our human potential. The expanded human encompasses all the hues of our being. All of the dark, the light, the bright, and the mystical. Each hue is essential and no hue is better or worse. They are all needed and all are important. We have always known this potential existed within us. It showed up in our dreams when we were children and flashed into our minds when we thought about giving up. It was the thing that propelled us to seek, and it was the thing that hid in the shadows of our fears. The secret is understanding there is no shortcut in this journey. Every second of the way is filled with information. We are no longer tantalized by the shiny things that promise it is all light, things we no longer need to feel sadness or experience darkness. We understand the need for balance between the light and the dark. Without one, the other wouldn't exist. The need to label things as good or bad leaves us. It's understood it is all here for us to experience. Discernment is present in our decisions and choices. All of it is there waiting so we can listen to what it is trying to tell us.

When our Soul yearns for more healing, the next step of the path is revealed. We are willing to look at and feel whatever we need to because we understand it is the way. We now have the ability to sit in our shadow and not fear it. When we try to avoid it or pretend it's something else, we miss the lessons. Fear holds pertinent information within. Embodied presence is our new experience. We are able to be present to what is. We understand our true needs. We do not question the perfection of the Universe, because we understand we are given what we need, when we need it. This doesn't mean it is easy. It's simply whatever it needs to be. Our part is taking that next step each day to meet what is waiting for us. We understand it's up to us to feed the hunger inside; to nourish it, to sit with it, and accept it. Whatever we are meant to experience that day is perfect. Presence is required to be able to receive the experience and information around us. When we need it to be something else, it is the very moment we fall into unconscious ego. But, we catch ourselves more often now.

Standing in our bodies, fully present to our feelings, we inhale fully and exhale a great noise. Within this noise is the Truth of our soul. Our unique humanism unapologetically expressed from deep within our being, with no guilt or shame. Our heart is now brimming with the love we spent a lifetime seeking from others. We are like a fountain of love, spilling out onto others. We are able to be present to all our splendors and all the tragedy in between. The gift of life is remembering our true Self, and the journey that takes us to this place is miraculous. Each and every step is required in order to unveil and shed the untruths that have kept us from living this way. No step can be skipped or bypassed; if it is, the lesson will be repeated until it's learned. We no longer need to change our state to a different one because we are now present to what is true, and we are ready for what life is bringing us. There is beauty in our friction, it's where we grow. Trusting in ourselves, and in Spirit, allows us to move through anything placed on our path.

When I look at the most challenging parts of my life, I now see they were the greatest opportunities. Within each challenging experience, a new tool or skill awaited. The joy was in who I would become, in figuring out how to move through it, and evolving to an expanded level of me. The self-mastery was in learning how to manage the reaction. Losing love, or the lack of intimate love, was always a trigger for me. It was the thing that would spin me into a state where I didn't know how to deal with my feelings. I always thought a lack of love was what made me not want to be here anymore. But when I could finally be present and listen, my true fear was revealed. I had a vision of me homeless on the streets, unable to take care of myself, with no money to eat, giving in to despair, and ending my own life. This was my true fear, that I couldn't love and care for myself. This fear had plagued my entire life; it was the thing that innately took me down and I repeatedly had to fight to come back from. Facing this fear was my greatest gift. It told me exactly what I needed to know to help myself. The vision showed me I had to do everything I possibly could to take care of myself. To prioritize my needs and to learn how to love myself. So I began to learn as much as I could.

Discovering more and more healing modalities, I traveled to Peru to learn how to be a practitioner of sacred Kambo medicine. I found I had the potential to aid others in their healing journey. The more I learned, the more I was able to take care of myself. They say our power lies in the parts of us we need to learn how to heal. My power came to me when I embraced the part of myself I had spent a lifetime running from. The journey of remembering me led to losing my fear of death. There is no end or beginning, simply transition. It's a continuous cycle. There is no shame for me in sharing my story. It's the journey I was given for my Soul to evolve. When I stopped fighting and trying to force my desires and wants, I was able to align myself with what is meant for me. There is a relief in letting go of what we have spent a lifetime fighting for, and in finding the beauty waiting for us within. My own materialism healed in this process. I no longer need to fill my life with things. This doesn't mean that I do not have what I need and don't enjoy the things I have, it simply means I understand the beauty in having enough and hope to support many others in finding this too.

The creative process used to stifle me. I was in such fear of how my offering would be received. I no longer fear what it takes to create. I am able to sit with and be present to the whole process. I attribute this to being able to sit in my shadows and feel what is there. I can create anything when I no longer have the need to try and make myself or the world different. Spirit brings through me what I am meant to share. I do not channel spirits or allow myself to be used as a vessel for things we do not understand; rather, I create from that place of the Divine, which we all have inside. This connection to a higher Self is about being present to only what is true. We all have our hero's journey. Each quest is exactly what our Soul needs to evolve. Your story and your evolution are not the same as mine; although underneath it all, we are the same! It is up to each and every one of us to find the way up our mountains, whatever that means for you. I believe this expansion of the Self is limitless. All you are searching for is waiting within you.

Creation said,
"I want to hide something from the humans until they are ready for it. It is the realization that they create their own reality."
The eagle said,
"Give it to me. I will take it to the moon."
The Creator said,
"No. One day they will go there and find it."
The salmon said,
"I will bury it on the bottom of the river."
The Creator said,
"No. They will go there, too."
The buffalo said,
"I will bury it on the Great Plains."
The Creator said,
"They will cut into the skin of the earth and find it even there."
Grandmother who lives in the breast of Mother Earth and who has no physical eyes, but sees with spiritual eyes said,
"Put it inside of them."
And the Creator said,
"It is done."
Creation story from the Hopi Nation, Arizona

TRUTH

Hueman! I can feel that fire inside of you that is waiting to ignite. What you are seeking can only be found deep within you; this life is about remembering our way back home. The current state of our planet and humanity is a catalyst to understand that the way we've been living isn't working.

What could we do with our human potential if we were deeply embodied in the truth deep inside of us? What kind of world could we create if the focus was not on money and success? What kind of humans could we be if we no longer needed to escape our lives and our feelings? Our human potential is not limited to the idea of a single dream. Our minds can dance with big ideas and flirt with questions that challenge the status quo.

It is time to ask ourselves bigger questions. What kind of world do we want to create, and what kind of people do we want to become?

This is the moment in time where we step away from the mundane and ask ourselves this - what do I have waiting inside of me? Remember how to access it.

This is a call for all trailblazers, galactic leaders, esoteric warriors, pirates, and potential Expanded Huemans. The expanded hueman within all of us is waiting to be remembered.

The Whole Method isn't telling you *how* to do things; it's reminding you that you have your OWN method. Your way, the way which will bring you back to Wholeness. The method back to wholeness requires us to face all the parts of ourselves. The person you have always known you could be is waiting for you in the darkest recesses of your Soul.

Jump in there, dear heart. Your true potential waits. The time is now. You are more powerful than you will ever know. You are being called to fully embrace your connection to Spirit, embody your wholeness, and take sovereignty over your own being. You are being called to remember your Truth. The Expanded Hueman community is waiting for you. Would you like to join us? Will you answer the call of your life?

Go to www.TheExpandedHueman.com/truth to sign up to our community.

You can also find us at www.facebook.com/groups/theexpandedhueman

"I am fascinated with human behavior and potential. My mind dances with big ideas and questions that challenge the status quo. What kind of world would we create if the focus was not on money and success? What would we do with our human potential if we were deeply embodied in the truth and ourselves?"

-RHONDA SMITH

CPSIA information can be obtained
at www.ICGtesting.com
Printed in the USA
FSHW020009031019